# White Saviorism and Popular Culture

This book interrogates the White Savior Industrial Complex by exploring how America continues to present an imagined Africa as a space for its salvation in the 21st century.

Through close readings of multiple mediated sites where Americans imagine Africa, *White Saviorism and Popular Culture* examines how an era of new media technologies is reshaping encounters between Africans and Westerners in the 21st century, especially as Africans living and experiencing the consequences of western imaginings are also mobilizing the same mediated spaces. Kathryn Mathers emphasizes that the articulation of different forms of humanitarian engagement between America and Africa marks the necessity to interrogate the White Savior Industrial Complex and the ways Africa is being asked to fulfill American needs as life in the United States becomes increasingly intolerable for Black Americans. Drawing on case studies from Barbie Savior (@barbiesavior) to *Black Panther* and *Black is King*, Mathers posits that global imperialism not only still reigns, but that it also disguises white supremacy by outsourcing Black American emancipation onto an imagined Africa.

This is crucial reading for courses on the cultural politics of representation, particularly in relation to race, social media and popular culture, as well as anyone interested in issues of representation in the global humanitarianism industry.

**Kathryn Mathers** is Associate Professor of the Practice in International Comparative Studies and Cultural Anthropology at Duke University. Her book, *Travel, Humanitarianism, and Becoming American in Africa* (2010) uses ethnographic observations of American travelers to southern Africa to ask why is Africa so important to Americans? She is co-producer of the documentary film *When I Say Africa* that challenges the image of Africa as a continent in need of saving.

**Routledge Focus on Media and Humanitarian Action**
Series editors: Robin Andersen and Purnaka L. de Silva

Humanitarianism is defined by assumptions that guide global solidarity, and posits that all peoples are part of the same humanity, no matter who they are, what they believe or where they live. These principles suggest that when media show the suffering of others, global publics respond in ways that facilitate disaster relief and help alleviate pain. But reactions to crises are also shaped by those who bear witness, tell the stories, share the data, and take the pictures of communities rocked by crises. Media content can also help those humanitarians who seek to address root causes of disasters, or it can serve to obscure the causes in many ways.

This series explores the multiple intersections between media and the work of humanitarian actors, and offers critical analysis of media, its uses, its coverage, how it has changed, and how it is misused in the representation of humanitarianism. Authors identify cutting-edge uses of new media technologies, including big data and virtual reality, and assess the conventions of older legacy media. For movements toward global peace, all peoples should be represented at the table and have their voices heard, including those outside the media spotlight.

**Al Jazeera, Freedom of the Press, and Forecasting Humanitarian Emergencies**
*Yehia Ghanem*

**White Saviorism and Popular Culture**
Imagined Africa as a Space for American Salvation
*Kathryn Mathers*

For more information about this series, please visit: www.routledge.com/Routledge-Focus-on-Media-and-Humanitarian-Action/book-series/RFMHA

# White Saviorism and Popular Culture
Imagined Africa as a Space for American Salvation

Kathryn Mathers

NEW YORK AND LONDON

First published 2023
by Routledge
605 Third Avenue, New York, NY 10158

and by Routledge
4 Park Square, Milton Park, Abingdon, Oxon, OX14 4RN

*Routledge is an imprint of the Taylor & Francis Group, an informa business*

© 2023 Kathryn Mathers

The right of Kathryn Mathers to be identified as author of this work has been asserted in accordance with sections 77 and 78 of the Copyright, Designs and Patents Act 1988.

All rights reserved. No part of this book may be reprinted or reproduced or utilised in any form or by any electronic, mechanical, or other means, now known or hereafter invented, including photocopying and recording, or in any information storage or retrieval system, without permission in writing from the publishers.

*Trademark notice*: Product or corporate names may be trademarks or registered trademarks, and are used only for identification and explanation without intent to infringe.

*Library of Congress Cataloging-in-Publication Data*
Names: Mathers, Kathryn, author.
Title: White saviorism and popular culture : imagined Africa as a space for American salvation / Kathryn Mathers.
Description: New York : Routledge, 2022. | Series: Routledge focus on media and humanitarian action | Includes bibliographical references and index.
Identifiers: LCCN 2022022007 (print) | LCCN 2022022008 (ebook) | ISBN 9781032112275 (hardback) | ISBN 9781032122588 (paperback) | ISBN 9781003223818 (ebook)
Subjects: LCSH: Humanitarianism—Political aspects—United States. | Group identity—United States. | African Americans—Relations with Africans. | Americans—Travel—Africa. | United States—Relations—Africa. | Africa—Relations—United States.
Classification: LCC DT38.1 .M365 2022 (print) | LCC DT38.1 (ebook) | DDC 303.4827306—dc23/eng/20220505
LC record available at https://lccn.loc.gov/2022022007
LC ebook record available at https://lccn.loc.gov/2022022008

ISBN: 978-1-032-11227-5 (hbk)
ISBN: 978-1-032-12258-8 (pbk)
ISBN: 978-1-003-22381-8 (ebk)

DOI: 10.4324/9781003223818

Typeset in Times New Roman
by Apex CoVantage, LLC

# Contents

*Acknowledgements* vii

**Introduction** 1

*Naming 4*
   *Reflecting on 20 Years of Imagining Africa 6*
   *A Brief Introduction to Sources 7*
   *Reimagining Africa 8*

**1 Traveling Images and How Americans Learned to Care for Africa** 15

*Traveling at the Millennium 15*
*Social Media and the Commodification of Caring 16*
*Voluntourism 17*
*American Encounters with Africa 19*
   *Change and Continuities 1999–2022 20*
*Making/Sharing Images 20*
*Learning/Curating Care 22*
*Seeing American/Seeing Race 24*
   *The Whiteness of It All 28*
   *Femininity, Consumption and Caring 29*
   *How To Become a White Savior 29*
*Lesson 1 – Love Africa 30*
*Lesson 2 – Love America 31*
*Lesson 3 – Save Africa 31*
*The Caring White Women Shopper 31*

## 2 The Barbie Paradox – How Parody Is Trying to Save Africa  42

*Celebrity Saviors 43*
*Seeing the Problem 45*
*Earnest Responses 46*
*Satirical Challenges 48*
*When Agencies Parody Agencies 50*
*Caring White Woman Shopping 54*
*When Africans Enter 55*
*Parody's Limits 56*
*Colonial/Postcolonial Entanglements 60*
*The Activist 61*
*Whiteness Winning 62*

## 3 Becoming American in Wakanda or Black is Queen  70

*Black Panther 72*
*The Film and Its Comic Book Inspiration 72*
*Zamunda 75*
  *The White Man's Burden 77*
*Coming From 'Africa Is a Country' 78*
*Beyoncé – African Goddess 79*
*The Gift 80*
*Black is King 81*
*African Artists/African Worlds 82*
*Imaging African Futures/Pasts 84*
*Un/Real Africa 86*
  *Saving America 88*
  *Unbearable Whiteness 89*
*Belonging in America 90*

## Conclusion  99

*Index*  109

# Acknowledgements

I am luckier than so many, as I navigated a global pandemic in a job that I could do at home, with a neighborhood 'home school' and family that stayed mostly safe in the US, South Africa and India. For the last ten years, I have been privileged to teach some amazing students in the Duke International Comparative Studies and Cultural Anthropology programs. They kept me thinking about how and why their desire to do good in the world was barely disrupted by their astute and critical understanding of the White Savior Industrial Complex and the tensions between caring about Africa and struggles over Black lives in the United States. They gave me the confidence to accept invitations by fabulous colleagues like Ami Shah to keep writing and thinking about how white Americanness continues to structure the saving Africa industry. A community of amazing women read, discussed and shared my work at International Studies and African Studies Association conferences. With support from thoughtful readers like Zeynep Gürsel, Sam Fury Childs Daly, Jehangir Malegam and great conversations and/or long walks with Grazina Bielousova, Jen Schaper, Sean Jacobs and Rebecca Stein I was able to take advantage of a year's leave to pull together a decade of wondering how and why we are still saving Africa for Whiteness. I am so appreciative for the thoughtful comments from reviewers and the close reading by editor Robin Anderson, who all took seriously what I was trying to do.

# Introduction

> I deeply respect American sentimentality, the way one respects a wounded hippo. You must keep an eye on it, for you know it is deadly.
> Teju Cole on Twitter, 2012.[1]

For nearly 25 years I have been keeping an eye on American sentimentality when it turned its eye on Africa. I am a white South African anthropologist of the United States, writing, thinking and teaching about Americanness, especially as it mobilizes Africa as a site for its redemption. I have heeded the warning in Teju Cole's tweet from his 2012 series on the White Savior Industrial Complex since beginning to observe American travelers to southern Africa at the turn of the millennium. As a white South African trying to understand the ways Americans were representing Africa, my Africanness has always been contested, disrupted and problematic. But my positionality as an outsider writing about the United States from the periphery is essential to how I respond to and understand the mediated visions and revisions of Africa in the United States. I see the sentiment and the effects of imaginings of Africa and Africans in the US as dangerous and unpredictable, just like a hippo – even when not wounded.

Here I think about these sentiments at two moments separated by roughly 20 years or so when Americanness has seemed most vulnerable and contested. This book is an opportunity to think through the ways that Americanness crafts itself in relation to Africa – what has changed and what has not in this time.[2] In my book *Travel, Humanitarianism, and Becoming American in Africa*[3] I argued that Africa became the space where Americans could find their better selves in the wake of 9/11 and the War on Terror. At a time when the world seemed to hate the United States, suffering Africans gave Americans a way to recreate themselves as good global citizens. Much of this was made possible by a set of images and narratives about Africa that evoked earlier colonial representational tropes. It (re)produced the White Savior

DOI: 10.4324/9781003223818-1

Industrial Complex that Teju Cole defined in a biting series of tweets in 2012 ending with his warning about American sentimentality quoted above. These tweets, expanded in Cole's subsequent article developed for *The Atlantic*, mark the shifting landscape of both these sentiments and the media that represent it.[4] Built into the stories of African hopelessness was a critique of the ways Americans were responding – should they be saving Africans and if not, then what should they be doing as Cole tweets: "5- The White Savior Industrial Complex is not about justice. It is about having a big emotional experience that validates privilege".[5] Despite the popularity of his challenge, much subsequent reflections on the white savior that I describe in this book disregard the imbrication between white saviorism and global capitalist and exploitative economies and institutions. I have been reminded, and remind myself and my students all the time, to include 'industry' and not simply reference white savior or a white savior complex. As Cole writes, white saviors "support brutal policies in the morning, found charities in the afternoon, and receives awards in the evening" as part of a set of systems and structures that go on whether the white saviors are present or not.

I want to understand what Africa means, at this critical juncture, to Americanness. Twenty years ago, travelers returning from southern Africa faced challenges to their ideas about belonging in America as the United States launched a 'war on terror' outside their borders. As I consider the meaning of Americanness today, Americans face another reckoning, one that is animated by violence from within rather than without. This reckoning heightened or framed perhaps by a global pandemic refracted events that might otherwise have gone unnoticed, as have so many violations of Black bodies in the United States over these last few decades. When George Floyd was choked to death on camera by police officers, Americans could not look away, and they were forced to watch as more and more such acts became forcibly visible to them. The United States and especially American Whiteness are being held accountable, much as American privilege was forced to look at itself post 9/11. The ways they are looking to Africa seem different on some levels, but other ways are all too familiar. This book explores the contested meanings of Americanness at these moments when it feels most wounded.

There are multiple sites at which these meanings are or can be negotiated. I have focused on representations of Africa and Africans in popular culture because as Ghanaian photographer Nana Kofi Acquah shows, much like American sentimentalism, imagined frames are dangerous:[6]

> When you are negatively represented in photographs, it becomes extremely difficult to move on, it's almost impossible, because to the world that is who you are, that is where you are, that is your country. That's what it is. You don't change. You don't grow.

In a conversation with Daniella Villasana in April 2020, Acquah articulated the danger of photographs that create a single story. They were discussing his viral Instagram post about the impact of COVID-19, calling out white journalists:

> Over 3,000 deaths in Italy, yet no graphic photos of the dying or dead.
> Dear White Journalists, can you photograph Africa with the same level of respect and empathy?
> Dignity is a fundamental human right, not the privilege of the few.

He is especially disgusted at the ways Sierra Leoneans, Liberians and Guineans were photographed during the Ebola pandemic in West Africa in 2014. The interview is accompanied by comparisons of Google image search results for COVID-19 and Ebola and searches for images of COVID-19 deaths and Ebola deaths. The Covid-19 images from around the world are mostly of the virus, lab researchers and multiple graphs with a few horrifying pictures of hospitals struggling to find spaces and mortuary staff transporting or burying completely wrapped up bodies. The Ebola images from West Africa were dominated by dead or dying bodes, clearly identifiable but not named, sick and weeping mothers with children or children waiting by their dead mother's side. Most are outside or being carried from shacks. The contrast is startling, but it is not surprising. As Acquah makes clear there is an all too familiar difference between the ways newspapers represent white tragedy and Black tragedy or Africa in general. He is not proposing that photographers start taking pictures of the white dead, but rather that they find a new way of portraying tragedy that does not so clearly make Black bodies a shorthand for violence and trauma.

This pandemic moment, just as I am trying to write again, about how and why images of Africa remain so consistent and damaging, is telling. While the images for COVID deaths in Africa are not so startlingly different from those for COVID deaths in the West, they are still more likely to show coffins, burial sites and unending lines for tests and vaccines. News photos have refrained from showing sick or dead Black bodies in the context of a global plague, but try as they have, journalists could not turn it into an 'African' plague. The confusion this created would be amusing if not so disheartening, as commentators struggled to find reasons grounded in something natural or biological to explain why the devastation of COVID-19 has not disproportionally hit African countries. Even in the self-critical news outlets in the United States, articles asked whether it was the weather, maybe some immunity garnered through living in poverty, or just the timing of the curve so the devastation would hit at any moment now.[7] Journalists struggled to acknowledge that many governments in Africa were able to manage prevention and produce a slower spread of infections. Despite a moment when so many people in the United States and Western Europe are questioning White privilege and even evoking the specter of global white supremacy, these same people fall back on tired stories and ideas about what Africa is and who lives there.

Representational tropes about Africa remain shockingly, yet unsurprisingly, unchanged despite the growing and equally persistent critique. Recent attempts to reimagine these tropes do not only marginalize Africans but also flatten out inequalities in the United States by drawing on ideas about Africa that ignore the geopolitical inequalities between the regions. This does harm to Africans of course in familiar ways, but it also does harm to Americans where both the privilege of Americanness and the violence it produces look like the same thing. I take my decades of teaching and observing and debating these ongoing erasures to consider what else was erased in this relationship – in particular the United States' global power and the mirrored elimination of American diversity.

Representations of Black Americans that tap into ideas about Africa often look very similar to those used to make Americans feel like only they can save Africa. Clive Gabay's exploration of early 20th century political imaginings of Africa makes a distinction between phenotypical Whiteness (physical skin color) and Whiteness, the totality of institutions and logics that control global politics and economics. These institutions incorporate their own justifications based in the genius of whites for their success and global power.[8] Gabay argues that Africa was and remains essential to maintaining the logic of white superiority. It is also able to incorporate narratives about Africa from people who identify as Black and/or African.[9] I am, therefore, also thinking through the consequences of media created to make Black Americans visible in popular culture and asking what it says about America. Ultimately, what does global Blackness mean when it is sited in the United States?

But while I examine this struggle to change perceptions and narratives about Africa, this is not a book about how to replace bad images with better images. I want to understand what my colleague Zeynep Gürsel has called the Humanitarian Industrial Complex and how it intersects with an Americanness that depends on the White Savior Industrial Complex.[10] By exploring some key moments in the popular culture motivated by desires to save or love Africa, I want to show how Americanness is articulated with Whiteness whether Americans are saving or celebrating Africa.

## Naming

In thinking about the way Africa is mobilized when Americans represent their place in the world, I trip over the very category I am describing. At the foundation of the critiques of the representations of Africa is exactly the problem of treating Africa as a singular and homogeneous space.[11] One of the key mechanisms for silencing all the diverse people who live and work in 54 African countries is to treat it as one place, so there are real dangers in trying to write about the idea of 'Africa'. For many there is no such thing as 'Africa' and no such thing as Africans, only Kenyans, Nigerians, Somalis, Zambians, etc. For others, Africa is an important idea about transnational political unity that includes not just people on the continent but multiple diasporas. The grouping of people as Africans holds other challenges, and in this context of articulating ideas of Africa with Americanness, I cannot use it as a simple replacement for Black. I must treat it as a descriptor of people and objects that live on, or are made or created, somewhere on the continent. I must ultimately use it in multiple ways: Africa as an imagined space on which much of the world imposes ideas about their own position in it; Africa as a geopolitical entity that is treated as a single unit by Western and Eastern powers in the interest of foreign policy and trade; Africa as an ancestral homeland where it is impossible to identify exactly where ancestors came from. This exploration has to be about a place called Africa because that is what I hear and see. It is how this place is almost always referred to, no matter what specific people or regions are engaged. It is the idea of Africa that is at stake here. I will only put it in inverted commas when its use is so egregious that the ridiculousness of it needs to be manifested.

Americans and America come with similar strictures. Why, as scholars and activists from Central and South America ask, are citizens of the United States the ones who get to call themselves Americans, though they are just one nation on these two vast continents?[12] I will try to call the place I write about the United States, but I also engage with an idea of who belongs there and the privileges that come with belonging, even when experienced in different ways through race and gender. It is also easy especially when thinking through popular media to conflate Americans and Westerners. The sites I examine, even the idea of the White Savior Industrial Complex, are produced by, consumed by, reflected and acted upon by people in western Europe as much as in the United States. It might not seem surprising that ideas about Africa in Europe and in the United States often look the same. My first book project began with the question about why American representations of Africa were so similar to European images that were grounded in colonial and postcolonial relationships. Yet this work showed that there is something recognizably specific as Americanness in the ways that citizens of the United States engage with and imagine Africa, not surprisingly given the different histories that tie the US to the continent, as well as contemporary US geopolitics.

## Reflecting on 20 Years of Imagining Africa

This book does something that scholars don't often get a chance to do, which is to build on a previous project. It is an opportunity to see a trajectory from then to now and reflect on how and why we have arrived here. This is the now familiar story of how Americans found themselves, and especially their better selves, in Africa that I wrote about in *Travel, Humanitarianism, and Becoming American in Africa* ten years ago. Based on an ethnography of American travelers to southern Africa I suggested and continue to argue here that Africa became necessary to the meaning of being American through an erasure of African specificity. Despite almost two decades of pop cultural reflection, criticism and viral social media about what it means to go to Africa to save or celebrate it, the continent and its people remain a space for Americans to find and save themselves. In this book, I will re-explore the research, ideas and interpretations I came to then to understand how Africa is manifest in today's youthful voluntourists.

The site of the paradox between critiques of white saviorism and the thriving White Savior Industrial Complex is made possible by the common tropes of representations of Africa in the West that have remained consistent into the 21st century – rural, silent, musical, primordial, primitive, focused on the past or on tragedies. Africa remains in the West's imagination as a single, homogeneous space with an imaginary geography rooted in colonial relationships.[13] As voluntourism was becoming a taken for granted element of making travel plans, Americans were watching documentaries 'about' Africans suffering, such as *The Devil Came on Horseback*; *Invisible Children*; *I Am Because We Are*; *War Dance*; *What are We Doing Here?* and *Virunga*.[14] These films did very similar work as 18th and 19th century popular writings that placed the European traveler at the center of their stage, thus dramatizing and eroticizing any contact between them and African people. The critical figure in these narratives is always the western adventurer whose journey to Africa, as the late art critic and curator Okwui Enwezor describes, "feeds an addiction – the fascination with Africa's ostensibly futile struggle to slip the clutches of a perpetual nightmare".[15]

Over the years social media and other pop culture sites have increasingly dominated discussions of the relationships I originally studied through participant observation of young American travelers to Africa. Alongside multiple conversations with students in global development and humanitarianism courses, I draw on a small selection of pop cultural sites that have animated debates with students and colleagues about the White Savior Industrial Complex and about representations of Africa in the United States, including parodic critiques as well as celebratory 'new' imaginings of Africa. Two decades ago, young Americans earnestly traveled to Africa to learn about what it meant to be American, a process that has turned into a set of viral memes, parodic and satirical critique and recently a site to celebrate Blackness. I try to understand how new generations of young critical Americans continue to travel to Africa to try to do good. I consider what harm is done when politics or worse, governance, and parody increasingly seem indistinguishable. At the heart of the analysis is this growing pop culture landscape of parody that simultaneously critiques and recreates representations of saving Africa.

## *A Brief Introduction to Sources*

I draw on blogs, memes, op-eds, film, music, humanitarian campaigns, and social media that have crossed my desk or that provide the fodder I use for pedagogy, classroom discussions and conference panels. I can make no claims to representivity, and no amount of deep diving into Twitter or Instagram can possibly scratch the surface of the diverse, strident or quiet and powerful voices that participate in the debates I am writing about. I follow the laughs to a large degree and notice what produced a conversation, an amusement or a debate as best I can on mediums that have no traditional catalogue. I am a sucker for network television, *Entertainment Weekly* magazine (in print), funny satirical skits my students share with me and the many, many thoughtful papers and challenges from my colleagues who care about the ways Africa is represented and what it means to Africans. The film, *When I Say Africa*, that I have been working on with Director Cassandra Herrman and Editor Linda Peckham for more than ten years, also provides a site of reflection, disruption and bewilderment. The tension between enthusiastic applause and dismissal raises productive questions about why it is so hard to change the conversation about Africa in the US. It forces a conversation about who is telling whose stories and why, and it opens up multiple provocative sites that tell us how Americans repeat their narratives, the stories about saving Africa that seem to end up in the same place they started.

I depend on the critical voices from the continent acknowledging that what I say here may undoubtedly be contested, debated and radicalized by activists, commentators, artists and writers all over Africa. I want this narrative to be as free as possible from citational genealogies, and so I write as freely as I can while offering a number of possible resources for more in-depth analysis and grounded research. The work I will share provides evidence that this is an active and impassioned space that I hope will at least be visible in my own attempt to figure out the lay of the land. I also draw on long term but intermittent fieldwork with the South African theater company Third World Bunfight to consider the ways Whiteness structures the relationships between the United States and Africa, even in spaces meant to represent Blackness. In a moment in history when Black bodies still need to be defended globally, is there any room left for a critique that originates from Whiteness, the space I must occupy?

## *Reimagining Africa*

When I started to work with filmmaker Cassandra Herrman on the documentary *When I Say Africa* more than ten years ago, representations of Africa were including this kind of self-correcting message but were being used to support a resurgent industry of saving Africa. The same old stories about the continent were being restyled by celebrities, now flowing over the new platforms of social media. More importantly there was clearly something very dark happening as ordinary Americans and famous ones rushed to find ways to demonstrate their love and care for Africa. Binyavanga Wainaina's essay on 'How to Write About Africa' published in *Granta Magazine* in 2005[16] spelled out the violence of the stereotypes about Africa circulating in the West, just when the White Savior Industrial Complex was remaking itself:

> Describe, in detail, naked breasts (young, old, conservative, recently raped, big, small) or mutilated genitals, or enhanced genitals. Or any kind of genitals. And dead bodies. Or, better, naked dead bodies. And especially rotting naked dead bodies. Remember, any work you submit in which people look filthy and miserable will be referred to as the 'real Africa', and you want that on your dust jacket. Do not feel queasy about this: you are trying to help them to get aid from the West.

In 2020 I curated an exhibit of photographs from the film.[17] *When I Say Africa* ends with a collection of photographs by artists from earlier generations like Malick Sidibé, Seydou Keïta and Soungalo Malé from Mali, Peter Magubane from South Africa and contemporary photographers working and living on the continent. Like anybody with access to the internet might, we found the photographs on social media sites, the artists' own websites and the Instagram account Everyday Africa, among others. The artists Hilina Abebe, Ethiopia; Arturo Bibang, Equatorial Guinea; Nana Kofi Acquah, Ghana; Barbara Minishi, Kenya; Andrew Esiebo and Fati Abubakar, Nigeria and Tina Zibi and Neo Ntsoma from South Africa have rich careers as photographers, journalists, artists, designers, and mediamakers on the continent and beyond. *When I Say Africa: Photographs from the Continent* was on display at the Duke University Rubenstein Arts Center in the first 2 weeks of March 2020.

At the entrance of the exhibit, a large poster sheet asked visitors to write responses to the question: "When I Say Africa, what do you think of?" Duke University students in a Documentary Studies 101 course and Introduction to African Studies also participated by writing individual responses to the same prompt. While follow up was shut down by the pandemic, the responses offer a glimpse into ideas about Africa in this moment when America is reframing its own sense of self.[18] While students and visitors come with various perspectives about Africa, the common elements suggested some overlapping themes, all too familiar from Binyavanga's essay. Their focus on violence and hopelessness alongside a kind of resplendent poverty remains consistent across the decades:

> I think of Africa like one of those destinations in a survival show on TV – not many resources and a harsh natural climate.
> 
> I see African people with brown skin, big smiles, amazing, unique, curly hair and prideful culture.
> 
> I think of the hot sun bearing down on scrawny African children. Dusty, dirty, poor, hungry people who are like hunter-gatherers. That sounds terrible reading it back to myself, but that's just the images I see.

Unlike Binyavanga's writers, this generation knows they need to question their assumptions and show a degree of self-awareness and critique that is a constant struggle in trying to reinvent the white savior. Here are some examples of these contradictions:

> I see white people spending their summer with black children and then posting mission trip-esque photos on Facebook and Instagram without the consent of those children.
> 
> Children in UNICEF ads/campaigns. Hungry/thirsty. Bellies swollen. Poverty. . . . White people in church groups exploiting said children in Instagram photos. But helping? . . . Confusion; a sense that the narrative I've always heard about Africa is overly simplistic [and] patronizing. A sense that my perception of Africa most of my life has been wrong.

But of course, not always:

> When I think of Africa, I think of the kids who despite having almost nothing, had everything. I went to South Africa as a sophomore in high school for a mission trip. There we visited a little school, an orphanage, and an AIDS camp. The kids at the school were always delighted to see us and welcomed us with open arms.

I will explore this paradox between self-awareness and the production of the same tropes about the continent in Chapter Two. But the most challenging aspect of making *When I Say Africa* has been the denial of the continuity of these tropes. As the film was coming together, we were struck by the inability to convey our perspective to fundraisers and documentarians who might have supported the film. While it was clear that our critique was recognized by others, we had always been sensitive to two challenges; the danger of reproducing the very images we were critiquing and possibly appearing to represent Africans. We were white filmmakers and writers interested in telling a story about western perceptions and the harm they do with the goal of giving those Westerners a chance to engage with their perceptions and assumptions in a productive yet critical space. No matter how often we renamed and restructured the film, we were always clear that this was a film about white people and an industry of knowledge and image production grounded in a global White supremacy and fundamentally about White privilege.

Yet no matter how clear most viewers of the film were that this was about them and their desires, funders remained insistent that there was a problem that Africans were not producing our film. No doubt, the marvelous films made by Africans that challenge the West's representation of their communities matter more. For example, Wanuri Kahiu whose 2018 film *Rafiki* was the first Kenyan film shown at the Cannes Film Festival; Kemi Adetiba, a Nigerian makes films for Netflix; Malian, Abderrahmane Sissako, directed the 2014 film *Timbuktu* that won awards in Cannes; Macherie Ekwa Bahango's, 2018 film *Maki'La* tells the story of street children in Kinshasa with no white savior in sight; Amjad Abu Alala made the Sudanese film *You Will Die at 20*; David Gitonga made *Nairobi Half-Life*; Katleho Ramaphakela, Tshepo Ramaphakela, and Rethabile Ramaphakela, produced *Seriously Single*; Ghanaian, Shirley Frimpong-Manso directed *The Perfect Picture*.[19] It, however, seemed to us as much our responsibility as anybody's, if not more so, to challenge the narrative white Westerners grew up with that drive us to engage with Africans in a particular way. This, I would argue, says everything about the problem with representations of Africa; there is only one story whether you frame it for good or carelessly in the context of White privilege and global White supremacy.

*White Saviors, Popular Culture and Saving America* asks how these contradictions make Americanness. While both the United States and the ways it imagines Africa have changed in some ways, the intersections between narratives and visual imaginings about Africa and belonging in America remain potent. In the early 2000s, as I argued in *Travel, Humanitarianism, and Becoming America in Africa*, the United States was reeling from the devastating attacks of 11 September 2001 and coming to terms with the idea that maybe they were not the heroes in a global story of good vs evil. Africa, with its horrifying HIV/AIDS epidemic devastating families and the lives of children, gave Americans a space to feel good. The popular culture at the time was unabashedly sentimental and unashamedly put the white savior figure front and center, leaving Africans to play sometimes beautiful and sometimes harrowing roles as minor characters in the background to their good works.

Two decades on and the United States is reeling again, this time from attacks on Black Americans and on the idea that they live in a country worthy of global respect. It comes with social media and a new wave of critical push back. Teju Cole's tweets have slowly eroded the simple narrative about African hopelessness and the possibilities for western people to save the day, especially through sentiment as he wrote: "3- The banality of evil transmutes into the banality of sentimentality. The world is nothing but a problem to be solved by enthusiasm".[20] Yet at the same time the industries that support white saviors thrive and multiply, even as those sentiments have become parody. The outcome is the same – Americans have continued to go to Africa to save it. Now popular films know better than to send white Americans to save Africans, but they have shifted to imaginings of Africa as central to telling stories about Black Americanness.[21] In these pages I want to understand what Africa now means, at this critical juncture, to Americanness.

This book is laid out in three chapters that draw from my past work and moves on to analyzing present conditions. I explore why Americans can't help themselves when they try to save Africa and seek to explain why this relationship is so important, especially at a moment when the US is coming to terms with its own deep history of anti-black violence. Each chapter stands on its own, but together they build a view of what it means to be a good American and how that intersects with the White Savior Industrial Complex. Over the last 20 years this dynamic has played out in popular culture by reinventing and representing Americans 'coming to Africa'. In each chapter I am in conversation with some critical writing about media forms that depict Whiteness and engage parody in various constructions of global Blackness.

Chapter 1, Traveling Images and How Americans Learned to Care for Africa, reviews the recent history of entanglements between Americans and the African continent. I use my field notes and student journals from ethnographic work with American travelers at the beginning of the millennium to think through how popular media reinvents ways to represent African helplessness. This has been essential for the formation of the 'good American' over the last 20 years in an increasingly neoliberal United States. I show how ways to save yourself by saving Africa have expanded to incorporate voluntourism and compassionate consumption. I argue that learning to love and care for Africa has been feminized in ways that allow critiques of the White Savior Industrial Complex to exist alongside and be entangled with the successful and growing White Savior Industry.

Chapter 2, The Barbie Paradox – How Parody Is Trying to Save Africa, unpacks the relationship between the ever-growing voluntourism industry and sites of parodic critique of the White Savior Industrial Complex, from Radi-Aid's Band Aid-like music video calling on Africans to send radiators to freezing Norwegians to the viral Barbie Savior Instagram account, @barbiesavior. I suggest that the satirical manipulation of visual, especially photographic, representations of voluntourism is neither as paradoxical as it seems, nor has it been an effective catalyst for creating new ways to see Africa. These sites of critique that replace sentiment with parody work to create an ideal White Savior Industrial Complex for an America that has to reckon with its own faltering status on the world stage. The ways satirical critiques and doing good go together only highlight how Americanness works successfully to entangle those with power and those without into a single space.

In Chapter 3, Becoming American in Wakanda or Black is Queen, I ask what is Africa to Americanness when American musician Beyoncé declares herself the universal African mother and when King of Wakanda comic book hero, T'Challa, dismisses the whole of colonized Africa as essentially lost. The stunning characters in films like *Black Panther* and *Black is King*, whose fashions appropriate an eclectic range of contemporary and historical African styles, offer liberation and beauty grounded in Blackness. These sites of American Black empowerment, however, depend on very similar tropes as those that create the White Savior Industrial Complex by sending Africans to the background of American lives. Their possible power as counternarrative to familiar representations of Africa obscures what it means to imagine an uncolonized Africa as the only way to emancipate Blackness. By asking who Africa belongs to in these representations, I explore the ways that Americanness articulates with Whiteness, implicating all Americans in the White Savior Industrial Complex.

I write as an anthropologist of America, as a befuddled scholar who continues to want to understand how and why society in the United States makes possible, supports and even celebrates a patronizing, neocolonial and even imperialist relationship with Africans. Ultimately, I believe that these funny, heartwarming and sometimes emancipatory sites of media production do more harm than good. I suspect producers know this already, and so I want to understand what good it does and for whom. I very much appreciate and enjoy the parodies, commentaries and films that I engage with here, though some do make me angry. These decades of critical and analytical sharp, funny, horrifying and beautiful music and films that try to reinvent how Americans see Africans and themselves have failed to change America's relationships to the continent or the relationship between the United States and Black Americans.

## Notes

1. Cole, Teju. 2012. 'The White-savior Industrial Complex.' *The Atlantic*, March 21.
2. I am deeply indebted to Ami Shah for her encouragement and critical reading and engagement with my work. She has introduced me to many fantastic women scholars who think seriously about what is funny (and not) about humanitarianism and images of Africa. I would also like to thank the reviewers who took seriously what I was trying to do and offered important insight into framing this book.
3. Mathers, Kathryn. 2010. *Travel, Humanitarianism and Becoming American in Africa*. New York: Palgrave.
4. Cole, Teju. 2012. Ibid.
5. Cole, Teju, 2012. Ibid.
6. Villasana, Danielle. 2020. 'The Baggage that Lives with You Forever: Photographer Nana Kofi Acquah on the Ethics of Imaging a Pandemic.' *R-Picture: A Publication of the Everyday Project*, April 1, 2020. https://medium.com/re-picture/the-baggage-that-lives-with-you-forever-15a86c3d4b93. Accessed September 12, 2021.
7. See for example: Baker, Aryn. 2020. 'Why Africa's COVID-19 Outbreak Hasn't Been as Bad as Everyone Feared.' *TIME*, December 30, 2020, 7:00 AM EST. https://time.com/5919241/africa-covid-19-outbreak/. Accessed September 12, 2021; The Economist. 'Why COVID-19 Seems to Spread More Slowly in Africa: Transport Links Are Worse.' *Johannesburg*, May 16, 2020. www.economist.com/middle-east-and-africa/2020/05/16/why-covid-19-seems-to-spread-more-slowly-in-africa. Accessed September 12, 2021; Soy, Anne. 2020. 'Coronavirus in Africa: Five Reasons Why COVID-19 Has Been Less Deadly than Elsewhere.' *BBC News*. www.bbc.com/news/world-africa-54418613 8 October 2020. Accessed September 15, 2021.
8. Gabay, Clive. 2018. *Imagining Africa: Whiteness and the Western Gaze*. New York: Cambridge University Press.
9. Gabay, Clive. 2018. Chapter 6: 'Afropolitanism and the White-Western Incorporation of Africa' In *Imagining Africa: Whiteness and the Western Gaze*. New York: Cambridge University Press: 182–202.
10. In conversation with Ami Shah, Zeynep Gürsel, Ellie Lapp, Alexandra Budabin, Adia Benton and Lisa Ann Richey on the panel, *The Humanitarian in the Mirror: Producing, Consuming, and Reusing Humanitarian Representations of the Global South*. International Studies Association Baltimore 22–25 February 2017.
11. Achille Mbembe called out the numerous ways Africa is constituted as one in his introduction here: Mbembe, Achille. 2001. *On the Postcolony*. Berkeley: University of California Press.
12. Martinez-Carter, Karina. 2003. 'What Does "American" Actually Mean?' *The Atlantic*, June 19, 2013. www.theatlantic.com/national/archive/2013/06/what-does-american-actually-mean/276999/; Martinez, Elizabeth (Betita). 2013. 'Don't Call This Country "America" How the Name Was Hijacked and Why it Matters Today.' *Z Magazine*, August 1, 2003. https://zcomm.org/zmagazine/dont-call-this-country-and-quot-america-and-quot-by-elizabeth-martinez/.
13. See for example: Brantlinger, Patrick. 1985. 'Victorians and Africans: The Geneology of the Myth of the Dark Continent.' *Critical Inquiry*, 12: 166–203, Gikandi, Simon. 1996. *Maps of Englishness: Writing Identity in the Culture of Colonialism*. New York: Columbia University Press, Harting, Heike. 2008.

'Global Humanitarianism, Race, and the Spectacle of the African Corpse in Current Western Representations of the Rwandan Genocide.' *Comparative Studies of South Asia, Africa and the Middle East*, 28: 61–77, Hibbert, Christopher. 1982. *Africa Explored: Europeans in the Dark Continent, 1769–1889*. London: A. Lane, Hickey, Dennis and Kenneth C. Wylie. 1993. *An Enchanting Darkness: The American Vision of Africa in the Twentieth Century*. East Lansing: Michigan State University Press, Keim, Curtis A. 1999. *Mistaking Africa: Curiosities and Inventions of the American Mind*. Boulder: Westview Press, Lutz, Catherine and Jane Lou Collins. 1993. *Reading National Geographic*. Chicago: University of Chicago Press, Mayer, Ruth. 2002. *Artificial Africas: Colonial Images in the Times of Globalization*. Hanover and London: University Press of New England, Nederveen Pieterse, Jan. 1992. *White on Black: Images of Africa and Blacks in Western Popular Culture*. New Haven, CT: Yale University Press, Peterson-Del Mar, David. 2017. *African, American: From Tarzan to Dreams of My Father – Africa in the US Imagination*. London: Zed Books, Wheeler, Roxann. 1999. 'Limited Visions of Africa: Geographies of Savagery and Civility in Early Eighteenth-century Narratives.' In *Writes of Passage: Reading Travel Writing*, ed. James Duncan and Derek Gregory, 14–48. London and New York: Routledge.
14. Fine, Sean and Andrea Nix. 2007. *War Dance*. Rogues Harbor Studios, Fine Films (II), Shine Global, Klein, Brandon, Klein, Daniel and Nick Klein. 2008. *What Are We Doing Here?* Klein Pictures, Mansour, Carol. 2006. *Invisible Children*. Invisible Children, Rissman, Nathan. 2008. *I Am Because We Are*. Semtex Films, Stern, Ricki and Anne Sundberg. 2007 *The Devil Came on Horseback*. Break Through Films, Von Einsiedel. 2015. *Virunga*. Grain Media, Violet Films.
15. Enwezor, Okwui. 2006. *Snap Judgements: New Positions in Contemporary African Photography*. London: Steidl/ICP, p. 15.
16. Wainaina, Binyavanga. 2005. 'How to Write About Africa.' *Granta*, 92(Winter). www.granta.com/Magazine/Granta-103/Letter-From/1.
17. This exhibit was funded by The Josiah Charles Trent Memorial Foundation Endowment Fund, the Duke Africa Initiative and the Rubenstein Art Center at Duke.
18. A Duke undergraduate research assistant, Molly Mendoza, did much of this analysis, and I am so appreciative of her reflective engagement with this material.
19. Abderrahmane, Sissako. 2014. *Timbuktu*. Les Films du Worso, Dune Vision, Arches Film, Adetiba, Kemi. 2018. *King of Boys*. Kemi Adetiba Visuals, Alala, Amjad Abu. 2019. *You Will Die at 20*. Andolfi, Canal+ International, DUOfilm. Bahango, Macherie Ekwa. 2018. *Maki'La*. Orange Studio, Frimpong-Manso, Shirley. 2009. *The Perfect Picture*. Sparrow Production, Gitonga, (Tosh) David. 2012. *Nairobi Half-Life*. One Fine Day Films, Ginger Ink Films, Kahiu, Wanuri. 2018. *Rafiki*. Big World Cinema, MPM Film, Schortcut Films, Mawuru, Godwin and Tsitsi Dangarembga. 1993. *Neria*. Media for Development International, Ramaphakela, Katleho and Rethabile Ramaphakela. 2020. *Seriously Single*. Burnt Onion Productions.
20. Cole, Teju. 2012. Ibid.
21. See this essay that explores the way white sentiment as expressed by Barbie Savior constrains white imagining of Black lives that Black Panther unleashes: Yeagley, Steve. 2018. 'Woke Worship: Taking Black Panther and Barbie Savior to Church.' *Spectrum*, May 4, 2018. https://spectrummagazine.org/article/2018/05/04/woke-worship-taking-black-panther-and-barbie-savior-church.

# 1 Traveling Images and How Americans Learned to Care for Africa

## Traveling at the Millennium

A young college student, visiting Cape Town as part of her summer immersion class on South African politics in 1999, is caught by surprise by an art piece in the South African National Gallery. The work, a collage titled 'Business' by the German South African artist Manfred Zylla, is a series of increasingly broken-down self-portraits of the artist in business attire. In each photograph his tie becomes more and more untangled, eventually seeming to strangle him. According to the student's journal, the artwork has a rather quirky and funny character, yet one that ultimately offers a dark critique of colonialism and especially capitalism. She is surprised that humor could be used to make such a serious criticism. She is not alone among her fellow study abroad students and other travelers. While they loved the stand-up comedians that they watched in Cape Town and Johannesburg, they were surprised at the biting approach to serious issues like racism, wealth inequality and the HIV/AIDS epidemic ravishing South Africa in the early 2000s. Rereading these journals 20 years later, these moments of surprise jump out at me as humor is now a taken for granted site of political critique for Americans. At the beginning of this millennium young travelers evoked sentiment and love to describe their experiences in 'Africa'. Now they rely on parody and satirical humor to try to understand the world.

In 1999 I began to follow travelers of all ages, but especially young study abroad students from the United States to southern Africa. Along with allowing me to interview them and hang out with them in South Africa and the United States, they shared their journals, printed photographs and written blogposts where they discussed their transformational experiences. They did this at a time before social media, when they did not have access to contemporary forms of digital travel or instant sharing opportunities and before voluntourism was a thing. These travelers discovered their identity as Americans in Africa. But they began their journeys when narratives about Africa

DOI: 10.4324/9781003223818-2

focused on its new democracies and capitalist economies and the United States seemed like a positive force in the world. However, by the early 2000s, the HIV/AIDS epidemic was dominating news in the West about Africa and 11 September left many Americans questioning their status in the world. While many of the travelers I worked with searched for career opportunities in the United States that had social value, such as labor movements, human rights law and immigration law, these events would lead Americans to turn to Africa as a place to salvage their sense of being 'good Americans'.

When I described this research in the book *Travel, Humanitarianism, and Becoming American in Africa*, published in 2010, I explored how travelers from the United States were motivated by their experiences in Africa to think critically about their own role in the world and the structural injustices that defined that historical moment, especially in Africa.[1] I argued that the idea of Africa that is shaped by travel has also helped create the logic of humanitarian aid and the sensibilities of the aid worker. But in the years between my fieldwork and publishing the book, Americans were reinventing both 'travel' and ways of doing good in the world. This reinvention began with the explosion of celebrity humanitarianism as famous people traveled to Africa to talk about how bad things were and to show themselves doing good deeds, like handing out mosquito nets and medications. Over the next decade, learning to care for Africans quickly became a western travel industry and an image and brand building business.

We live in a world saturated with visual images and so perhaps take for granted both their benign-ness and their power. Images have the power to shape – not only reflect – our world.[2] Let's imagine then what such a world might look like where images substitute for lived experience, as they can through social media, creating a geography almost entirely represented by visual spaces. The world for many young travelers and volunteers today is made of such visual geographies. It is not surprising then that much of these differences between Americans trying to save Africa today compared to 20 years ago lies in the ways their participation is mobilized through visual landscapes. The COVID pandemic may change travel and humanitarian industries. My work with mediated spaces that make armchair travel almost continuously possible, and the ways social media sites create the same kind of unequal relationships, however, suggest that we cannot depend on structural barriers to travel changing the ways, imagining and engaging with Africa centers a White Savior Industrial Complex in the United States and Western Europe.

## Social Media and the Commodification of Caring

*Travel, Humanitarianism, and Becoming American in Africa* ends just as ways of doing good in Africa adopt two substantially new forms – shopping for good and voluntourism. These developments rendered humanitarian activities and sensibilities sites for consumption and caring that make and sustain the White Savior Industrial Complex so devastatingly characterized by Teju Cole.[3] This is politics, disguised as sentiment, grounded in North American and Western European desires to continue extracting resources from African nations while offering humanitarian rather than political or economic structural reform in return.

The rise of social media offered new ways of 'doing good', and quick and easy mediated ways of demonstrating care became readily available online, creating a new form of activism, clicktivism or even slacktivism.[4] Caring about something or someone simply required changing your profile picture or using appropriate hashtags to make political statements. In the early 2000s Bono launched the (RED) campaign on the Oprah show beginning a massive highly mediated campaign to associate doing good with shopping.[5] (RED) is an ongoing campaign that enlists celebrities in its message to western consumers to "shop until it stops". It partners with high-end brands such as Apple, Armani, American Express, Gap, Converse and Hallmark among others, who donate a percentage of a purchase of a 'red product' to the Global Fund. It quickly became a taken for granted way to be a humanitarian. Shopping for good or compassionate consumption proposes that a good consumer of the right products can stay at home while simultaneously doing what previous generations had to travel to the village to do – gaze on, penetrate or save.[6] The BOGO (buy one give one) juggernauts like TOMS shoes and Warby Parker sunglasses are just a couple of the multiple brands whose business/marketing model is founded on telling their customers that for every pair of shoes or glasses they buy, a pair goes to someone in need. These current humanitarian impulses not only fit comfortably within neoliberal ways of being but remain articulated with the classic tropes of images and ideas about Africa that position Africans as hapless victims waiting for help and food to be given to them by the affluent and generous consumer culture of the West. I suggest that, while we did not have the tagline for the White Savior Industrial Complex (WSIC) years ago, this relationship of who gets to be a savior or carer and who needs to be saved remains depressingly the same.

## Voluntourism

Travel, whether in person or via a mediated gaze, has functioned for centuries as a way of articulating western power and authority in and on Africa. Through the 19th and 20th centuries, travel or at least the writing about travel gave Europeans and Americans opportunities to face their own savagery and to create an idea of Europe and North America as places that had tamed these dark impulses. In this century, the rise of social media quickly became a powerful tool to take Americans into worlds that they might never visit themselves – a digital version of the 19th century armchair traveler's dependence on explorers serializing their encounters in newspapers.

There is a long history of sending Americans and Europeans to poor countries or even to poor areas in their own countries. In the US agencies like the Peace Corps and TeachAmerica continue to thrive. The idea that volunteering could enhance holiday travel got its celebrity name around 2014.[7] Voluntourism serves to market and commodify 'doing good' and merge it with travel, turning volunteering into a professional development tool. Organizations like World Nomad, DiscoverCorps and GVI offer opportunities to save turtles or rhinos, help orphans or farmers or build wells and libraries in Kenya, Costa Rico, Peru, etc. while also going diving, hiking or on safari. These trips can cost anything from about $1800–$5000 for a few weeks. A 2008 survey of 300 organizations that market to would-be voluntourists estimated that 1.6 million people a year volunteer on vacation, spending around $2 billion annually.[8] By 2014, as many as 10 million volunteers a year were spending up to $2 billion on the opportunity to travel with a purpose.[9] In 2019 the predictions were for a booming 2020 year for voluntourist organizations, a prediction that was bamboozled by the COVID pandemic. Recent numbers of voluntourists worldwide are hard to find. Industry insiders seem to agree that this is a constantly growing business and is supported by trends toward eco-travel and other culturally sensitive approaches to tourism.[10]

By the second decade of the 21st century, this growing voluntourism industry testifies to the almost complete acceptance and indeed merger of travel and humanitarianism, defining a new role for Westerners – the voluntourist, a person who can travel for fun and for good all at the same time. Instead of exposing western structural power, travel has intersected with the aid and humanitarian spaces of control, serving rather to obscure the work of extractive and imperial relationships.[11] The images that encourage and support traveling to Africa to do good, though as multiple and diverse as Africans are, ensure that the foundational narrative of humanitarianism remains in place – that there are only intermittent crises and simple solutions to the problems faced by Africans. Despite the good intentions on which voluntourism is built, these travelers are following well-worn pathways in taking up the burden of global power by going to Africa to save Africans.

Here I will go back to my own ethnographic research at the beginning of the millennium with young Americans who traveled to southern Africa. I put their experiences together in conversation with highly mediated voluntourism experiences. I will show the continuities and differences between travelers two decades ago and contemporary voluntourists and clicktivists today. I seek to understand how the voluntourism industry and the broader tropes of 'helpless Africans' bloomed alongside a popular culture that seems politically astute and self-critical.

## American Encounters with Africa

Around 1999 and 2000, long before voluntourism dominated conversations in high schools and colleges in the US, I conducted ethnographic fieldwork with young American travelers to southern Africa, including some taking part in the then largely nascent volunteering opportunities. All the study abroad programs I worked with included a service component, which might seem obvious now but in fact was rather strange in the context of study abroad at the time. It was primarily in these Africa programs that students embarking on an opportunity to take classes and study toward their degree in a foreign country were also asked to be volunteers in social, often education, programs. Study abroad to Australia, Italy, Chile, etc. did not automatically offer such programming. A year or two after their travels to southern Africa most of these students had found a way to understand their experiences in South Africa as a journey toward learning to help Africans. In essence they reinvented the most recent shape of a long history of Euro-Americans saving Africans.[12] Just as there was no voluntourism industry or service-learning credit associated with the journeys of young Americans at the turn of the millennium, there was little overt critique or parody of their experiences. Sentiment and the discourse of a love affair could characterize their narratives, not self-conscious parody.

Since conducting this intensive fieldwork, I have been teaching and mentoring students as they planned research and travel in Africa. My writing has continued to engage with media and research on traveling to do good, as I tried to grasp the spaces Africa occupies on social media for young do-gooders.[13] I have also been workshopping the film *When I Say Africa* with wide ranging audiences of college students and K-12 teachers and students.[14] I rely on this work and experience as well as recent published studies of voluntourists. This fast-growing body of research offers insight into the ways that international volunteering is narrated in the lives of young people themselves, as well as by others engaging with their social media profiles.[15] This contemporary group of young Americans and Europeans who want to save Africa exist primarily in a world dominated by social media through which they have constructed a collective society that empowers them to define their own identities and to portray how they wish to be seen.[16] They are also a lot more self-critical and cynical about what they are doing than the travelers I worked with.

## Change and Continuities 1999–2022

As I re-explore the journals and field notes I accumulated over 3 years of fieldwork between 1999 and 2001, I am struck by how much and how little things have changed. I focus here on the observations of students on a summer political science course that spent a month in Cape Town and Johannesburg after class work in California in 1999 and 2000. They are illustrative and echo many of the more detailed stories that I tell in *Travel, Humanitarianism, and Becoming American in Africa*. While in South Africa these students met various parliamentarians, generally leaning left as members of the African National Congress and the Democratic Party, as well as activists, organizers, former political prisoners and artists. Every student chose to focus on different aspects of their journeys in their journals and to describe different encounters and experiences framed by their own lives and expectations for the course. Here I curate some examples of common narratives. As with anything we reread, I respond to them very differently than I did when reading them 20 years ago. The current context shapes the moments that jump out at me, structured as it is by the conversations I have in class and through social media with young Americans who are coming face to face with explosive debates and real-life crises around gender, race and class in the United States. Their passions and concerns are both deeply and profoundly grounded in United States history but intersect with global worlds, whether they are debating LGBTQ+ activism, global White supremacy, the impact of Black Lives Matter beyond US borders or the disproportionate impact of COVID on the American and world poor. Earlier generations were also struggling with many of these questions, though in different kinds of community spaces, and I want to explore as best I can the ways caring for Africa has or has not changed.

## Making/Sharing Images

The ever-present camera/camera phone is certainly the most common denominator across these generations. Travelers are told to be respectful when taking photographs, yet they rarely hesitated to snap an image of whatever caught their interest.[17] I seldom saw tourists or study abroad students approach people to ask if they could take a photograph. Some tried to challenge their classmates, as one student in 1999 writes here about fighting with a classmate who took video without permission, even dismissing her objections as an illegitimate claim to speak for "her" people:

> I cannot believe his lack of respect. It is as if the African people are not capable of being given the choice to make their own decisions. This paternalistic view that my classmate possesses is a remnant of

white supremacy which is so ingrained in his psyche that he ceases to acknowledge or even understand it exists within himself.

Despite the occasional twinge of doubt or challenge from a more aware classmate, the travelers' focus was on recording evidence of the exotic in the places they visited or among the people they saw, and this required, it seems the subject's lack of awareness.

Study abroad students in Kenya during a 2000 trip, for example, would rather take photographs from the safety of their vehicle or otherwise at a distance if they thought they could get a serendipitous shot of a young Maasai initiate or other unsuspecting person going about their 'traditional' business.[18] They were horrified when asked for payment for the privilege of taking images of anybody who they thought was performing a role. Fifteen years later this same impetus played out in a slightly more sophisticated way among voluntourists interviewed by Kaylin Schwarz. They actively avoided posting images that disturbed the expectations of what was African or indeed Maasai.[19] They worked hard to perform or stage a recognizably authentic encounter, even while being aware of the difference in the lives of many people from these representations. Both generations strove to capture that one image that said 'This is Africa'. They, therefore, rejected images of everyday life that made clear the contemporaneity of Maasai lives or the extent to which host families lived thoroughly embedded in what their peers back home would perceive as western lifestyles. Travelers self-censored and monitored their use of images, as well as the way they took pictures.

Another echo in 2000 of what was to come in social media saturated travel is the ways travelers preferred to show me photographs of friends and host families, social events, parties and dinners marking the passage of time and the development of life-long friendships while abroad. While in South Africa they sought out the perfect encapsulation of 'coming to Africa', back home they often only displayed or talked about the pictures of friends, classmates, or teammates illustrating their adventures and social lives while in southern Africa. Most of the photographs were/are meant to tell the story of a traveler's experiences, as well as reflect the sentiments that led them to take on the challenges of traveling in Africa. Ruth Cheung Judge's work with young British people from ethnic minority and disenfranchised backgrounds who take volunteer trips to southern Africa importantly shows the power of fun and even short-lived friendships to disrupt the neocolonial relationship between western saviors and Africans.[20]

Nevertheless, images mostly recreate these very inequalities, especially in the now ubiquitous photographs of American or European visitors surrounded by young brown or black children. This shorthand for caring is familiar not just from individual blogs (back then), social media pages and personal spaces, but in the humanitarian and development industries' fundraising, promotional and reporting materials.[21] Every traveler I worked with had albums and frames full of photos of posing, grinning and waving children. Possibly this is because they are the archetypal image of the continent, the one most often spoken of before arriving in 'Africa' and the one most often seen in news media in the US – a shorthand for authentic Africa and a caring westerner all in one. Not all young travelers were blind to the problem of taking these photographs. One college student in 1999 described how uncomfortable she felt when her classmates insisted on taking a rather awkward forced (paid) photograph with kids who appeared unwilling and unhappy:

> That night, I really felt like I wanted to be away from the people I was with because the whole thing made me feel so bad even though I know they had good intentions.

Despite such perspectives and the subsequent criticism and parody of these images, children are equally common accessories in recent iterations of representing travel to Africa and most importantly the value of volunteering in Africa.[22]

## Learning/Curating Care

Voluntourists today head to Africa having already learned to care and to see themselves as the appropriate vehicle for caring. Earlier generations, however, were still learning to inhabit this role, questioning their purpose as another student in Cape Town 2000 writes:

> I feel so useless at Akani [Community school in Masiphumelela, Cape Town]. We attempted to teach the children some English and grammar today. I have absolutely no idea how to teach English. Just because I know how to speak English doesn't mean I know how to teach it.

They would discover the desire to help Africa mostly after their return:

> I definitely have a lifetime interest in aiding in the future development of South Africa. After talking to so many interesting people and seeing so many beautiful children in the townships I want to do something to help them realize their dreams. It's unbelievable the position of privilege that we occupy as American citizens.

Fifteen to 20 years later voluntourists navigate a keen sense of the problems with traveling to Africa to save it. They are familiar with the abundant critiques of doing good abroad through both academic and popular sources. Pippa Biddle, who exploded into the debate with her viral blog post in 2014 and is a key interlocutor in the film in post-production, *When I Say Africa*, represents this generation of questioning and critical volunteers. Pippa's post reflecting on her experience as a voluntourist in Tanzania, "The problem with little white girls (and boys): Why I stopped being a voluntourist",[23] struck a chord among young Americans who were enthusiastic participants in this booming industry. Not only did Pippa's story of realizing that her groups' efforts to build a library was an illusion revealed when local workers had secretly repaired the walls they 'built' the day before, but she questions who does this kind of volunteering and why it is needed in the first place. Pippa was brave enough to talk about race and white privilege before these became common hashtags. In one scene in the film, she asks a group of University of North Carolina Chapel Hill students if they would ever go to a park or a mall in the United States and pick up a child to take a photograph with. The response is largely some uncomfortable shifting in their seats at the silliness of the familiar gesture of gathering brown or black children around you to take a picture while abroad.

Such questions haunt contemporary voluntourists and my students planning (outside of a global pandemic) socially engaged travel. They think about popular critiques like those made by Kascak and Dasgupta[24] about instagramming Africa that describes three common tropes in volunteer photography: the suffering other (a saddened child with a distended belly), the self-directed Samaritan (a smiling volunteer surrounded by service recipients) and the overseas selfie (a close-range, self-composed photograph of the volunteer). Students agree with Kascak and Dasgupta argument that these self-presentations represent "an imaginary geography whose landscapes are forged by colonialism, as well as a good deal of narcissism". Yet they are often reading these critiques in the context of planning their own voluntourism experience.

This tension, as well as self-awareness, was paramount in the honors thesis research of Duke International Comparative Studies student, Elsa Gunnarsdottir, conducted at the Moroccan Children's Trust in Taroudant. While working as a volunteer Gunnarsdottir interviewed other volunteers from North America and Europe and on-site coordinators.[25] Her interlocutors were not blind to the multiple and complex ways in which voluntourism can be a neocolonial project. The young women she interviewed or worked alongside were fully aware of the landscape rife with parody and both cultural and political critique of the 'white savior complex' and with a sophisticated and intriguing set of reasons for adopting this form of service. Yet the idea that they should still travel to Africa to help remains fundamental to representational politics and self-representation among these young Westerners.

It is not surprising, therefore, how meticulously voluntourists today curate their journeys and experiences abroad alongside their desire to show the 'real Africa'. Kaylin Schwarz describes how careful young travelers are of their self-representations, making sure that they did not suggest an overly congratulatory tone or suggested they thought of themselves as doing good.[26] In addition, they censored themselves through the critical lens on humanitarianism with which they were familiar and avoided showing the images that are so often mocked by comedians or late-night talk shows.

## Seeing American/Seeing Race

The travelers 20 years ago were wrestling in similarly contradictory fashion with some of the same questions about race in the United States and globally as Americans in the 2020s. They came face to face with their privilege, with racism both in South Africa and at home and with a sense of what it means to be American. First, they started to see that the United States and South Africa were perhaps not that different and in many ways are as conflicted about the United States and its racist history as their contemporaries today:

> In the end the differences I have noticed here blend into one observation: on a basic level we all struggle with the same problems. I found myself continually comparing South Africa with the United States to learn that on a very personal level it's all the same crap just a different set up. The question is how to go about chipping away at the problems that are always present in unequal societies.
>
> In a way, I think of South Africa as similar as parts of the Deep South where racial tension still exists. Because of the shift in public opinion away from favoring racial segregation and the general shift to disapproval of discrimination, racism has basically only been swept under the rug and buried in the back of people's minds.
>
> In America, it is easy for middle class whites to turn a blind eye toward this issue (Racial thinking). But this is a prevalent issue everywhere, one that is more common than many will admit.
>
> In the US I had always accepted racial categorizing for the sake of remedying racial inequalities. Here I must accept race is not just a category it is a distinction – and not a positive one.
>
> But perhaps the greatest realization I have had and the most disturbing one, is that race does truly matter, in this world. Before going to South Africa, I had been trying to convince myself that racism is dying in the United States, and that we can look at each other as human being.

However, others seem to see South Africa as that place with racism, whereas the United States is so much better as this student's diary entry about seeing a young girl getting her hair straightened shows:

> It just surprised me because I have never seen such a young child go through such a longer and involved process for their hair. To me, it just showed the lengths some people got to hide their roots. When she walked out, she could definitely 'pass for white'. It seems like the hierarchy is so ingrained into this society – everyone wants to be better than someone else's and upgrade themselves.

or

> Naturally I think about my own neighborhood in Oakland and how it is divided by ethnicity yet the lines of division are fairly fluid. I wonder if the lines dividing races in Cape Town will be strikingly visible.

Some understand from these similarities and differences that there is a certain privilege and matching responsibility to being a citizen of the United States:

> I have gotten to do all these things because by some accident of fate I was born in the world's wealthiest country at a time when a woman traveling the globe is not at all uncommon. There are many privileged American and European women wandering around the world with backpacks. I never lose sight of the fact that my travel is a way to learn about the rest of the world so that eventually I will be more able to help the women I have met and talked to on my travels. I believe that it is my duty as an American to find out about the world around me and to study the way that my very powerful country fits into the international community.
>
> I realized that anyone living in the United States, be it millionaire or a beggar, is lucky. They have opportunities that I find, so far, to be absent here. I think that compared to other nations, the United States has a wealth of organizations committed to the welfare and improvement of its people.

Their conviction that America is a country where 'multiculturalism' or a post racial model is successful is somewhat parsed by the students of color who draw on their own experiences, as well as international students and some more thoughtful students, who wonder just how much better things are in the United States. They do recognize that Black South Africans have harder economic challenges than Black Americans, but express confusion over how to understand the resentment from Black South Africans of

American privilege and are frustrated that the struggles of Black Americans are not recognized as similar to those of South Africans:

> (Black UCT students) suggested that Black Americans were not taking advantage of all the opportunities that they had available to them. They insisted that Black Americans had access to good schools, jobs, etc. I asked them if they considered the institutionalized racism in the United States as a possible reason that more Black people were not able to take advantage of opportunities and they think that it was not a real obstacle.
>
> Again, I was really upset at how we were treated because we were Americans. This man did not know me personally nor had he heard anything about me but because I was American I was treated badly. This is similar to how I am treated in the United States by other non-black races, because I am black I am treated different regardless of my character or class.
>
> Here where people who had been persecuted for at least half their lives based on the color of their skin-refusing to acknowledge a similar phenomenon in another country because it manifests itself different and in a less obvious way.

This is understood in part as a problem of representation:

> I came to the conclusion that this is the only image they have seen of Americans on television and magazines. We are portrayed as rich, stuck-up, picky inconsiderate, sex driven people who have no heart.

While frustrated that racism in the US does not offer Black Americans a shared space with many of the South Africans they meet, many students still suggest that the United States is ahead of the global game in addressing and dismantling racist structures.

Though, some white students talked about the doors at clubs and elsewhere that opened wide because they were both white and American. Others expressed a sense of their privilege as Americans but grounded this primarily in the conviction that this came solely from the superiority of the United States. Their country was fixed in their minds as a better society especially with respect to racism:

> In the US there is a very clear understanding of equality and the intolerance for racism. Consequently when outright actions of bigotry take place people are quick to stand up and defend their rights. However in South Africa the idea of equality is so new both Blacks and Whites are quick to fall back into their 'master and slave' complex.

Multiculturalism in the US celebrates this or at least celebrates all of the unique cultures/races that make up 'America'. This is good because they are certainly all valuable, and knowing/living ones' heritage is important. But it also continues to divide us.

The tone in general across these and many other travel journals and interviews is that they want to learn about this new democracy with its strange and incomprehensible racial politics so they can reflect on how lucky they are in a country that already 'does' democracy. Whether about the good or the bad these young Americans believed that South Africa could learn from the United States and that Americans can show South Africans how to make the world a better place. For some they wanted to do that work in the United States, for others they wondered if they should return to South Africa or to their ancestral family home in places like India. What jumps out to me though here is that 20 years ago young Americans were asking very similar questions about white supremacy, US hegemony and their role in the world, while also seeing themselves as saviors.

These critical, ambivalent, thoughtful but possibly naïve young people came home to what would soon become a 20-year 'War on Terror', but they also quickly found ways of expressing the lessons they learned about caring for Africa. This reflection from a student in 1999 lies closer to the ways the images of Africa reinsert themselves over the next two decades. Africa remains fixed as a place where Americans can find power and beauty in Blackness:

> I also see Africa as a place of rich culture. It is there where culture was invented and has influenced millions of people. My example of this is how many people in America wear African clothing and try to duplicate the culture of black Africans through song and dance. Africa must be a powerful place if it has this amount of influence on the people of America. I hope that during my stay I will be able to come in contact with this strong culture.

I retell these stories because in the intervening years important elements of this healthy state of confusion are flattened out. Experiences like the ones I observed in southern Africa very quickly become 'about' Africa in general and not a particular place.

The next generations do not hold onto the lessons about their privilege except in the sense that they feel responsibility for helping the less fortunate. This is the period I describe in my book when everybody was going to Africa to save it – Oprah, Angelina Jolie, Madonna, *American Idol*, a multitude of church groups, school-based mission organizations and college volunteer groups.

Universities like Duke established programs like DukeEngage[27] that offers paid-for volunteering opportunities around the world and in the United States. Can these intersecting points between then and now show how travel encounters that taught young Americans to recognize American power and privilege in the world became commodified practices – travel or shopping – that sustain a White Savior Industrial Complex entangled with its own critiques?

## *The Whiteness of It All*

Social media began to fuel these journeys, but then to replace travel, drowning out the ambivalence and confusion that the young travelers above struggled with. This trend reached its peak (trough) in 2012 with the release of the film *KONY 2012*. This 30-minute film was a social media call to arms offering an Action Kit (for a cost) to young Americans who wanted to rid the world of its most evil (according to the video) human being, the Ugandan warlord, Lord's Resistance Army (LRA) leader Joseph Kony. Made and released by the nonprofit Invisible Children, it practically broke the internet, becoming a phenomenon among everyday Americans and celebrities alike,[28] and making Joseph Kony the most hated man in America overnight. Invisible Children's founder, Jason Russell, had made a film of the same name in 2006 with his co-founders, Bobby Pailey and Laren Poole.[29] They had traveled to Gulu, Uganda planning to make a documentary film but with no clear idea of what it would be about. They found their subject when they 'discovered' thousands of homeless children in the city, victims of war in Central East Africa. These, they insisted, were invisible children – invisible to anybody but them, that is. They made the film based on the idea that nobody 'saw' these children and used it to found a fundraising organization supposedly to support them.[30] The viral video 6 years later, however, focused almost entirely on how the US needed to capture Joseph Kony, by then a not especially powerful figure in Uganda though the history of violence perpetrated by the LRA was indeed horrific.

*KONY 2012* was not about educating the American public about the region's history or current challenges but about creating a deeply sentimental call to action in the name of saving helpless children in a helpless and hopeless country. By call to arms, they meant, buy our kit, raise more money for us, wear the bracelet that says you care, plaster posters everywhere and change your profile picture to the *KONY 2012* logo so everybody knows you care. It was incredibly successful as a social media campaign and in fact got many people thinking that the solutions to Uganda's problems were to mobilize military forces to go capture Joseph Kony. Enough people believed this, in fact, that it did become a reality, though it fizzled out in 2017 when the US and Ugandan militaries declared Kony and his army irrelevant.[31] It is a master class in flattening out and simplifying Africa's problems but also offering a transactional neoliberal solution for young Americans to embrace. Its success was in many ways its downfall, as alongside the emotional breakdown of its creator, Russell, it was just too ridiculous for Ugandans to stay silent about, and the push back was real and impactful.[32]

This bizarre film, however, was very prescient in exposing the now entrenched system of helping Africans through the right kind of social media profile and through shopping. This is the engagement with Africa that is so bitingly parodied in the media sites I will be exploring in the next chapter. Here I want to think through how the earnest caring of the earlier generation and the complicated engagement with American privilege at the turn of millennium has turned into a shopping spree and what that says about Americanness.

## *Femininity, Consumption and Caring*

How has shopping for goods grown into a space where it remains possible to be a critical, informed white savior without really acknowledging the paradox between consumption and alleviating poverty? I will show that the gendering of shopping and especially shopping to care helps to sustain these contradictions in a generation that, unlike 20 years ago, knows all too well how imperialist their gestures to save Africa are.[33] By exploring how caring is feminized through shopping, I argue that by reinscribing the male and white gazes that made imperialist extraction possible onto humanitarian impulses, compassionate consumption succeeds in feminizing these unequal relationships and thus blurring the violence of the White Savior Industrial Complex.[34] At the center of these images and commodities I want to show here is a narrative of care that positions white women as the best avatars for the WSIC and, at the same time, the primary problem with it.

## *How To Become a White Savior*

This narrative of care, the gendering of who gets to engage with Africa and how and the idea that consumption of commodities but also of images and of experiences override any actual thoughtful need to engage with Africans themselves are birthed, I suggest, not in humanitarian engagement but in adventurous explorations. Nearly 15 years ago Laura Hubbard and I wrote two essays on the ways Americans were imagining and engaging with Africa that highlight how this 21st century generation of white saviors learned to care for Africa.[35] Our sites of study were adventure tourism – bungy jumping at Victoria Falls, white river rafting down the Zambezi, and the then only third season of the reality television juggernaut, *Survivor*

*Africa* (first aired on CBS 2001). This site in particular offers an armchair voyage to Africa made possible by mainstream US media that introduced a way to love and care for Africa to a new generation of Americans. This narrative would later appear on multiple media sites from *American Idol* to *E.R.* (when Americans still watched network television).[36] While media doesn't create these relationships, *Survivor* reveals the language and ideas that would influence in disturbing ways how young Americans engaged with Africa. Adventure and penetrative action made it possible for the discourse of care to dominate northern relations with the continent as Binyavanga Wainaina's essay so perfectly describes:

> Africa is the only continent you can love – take advantage of this. If you are a man, thrust yourself into her warm virgin forests. If you are a woman, treat Africa as a man who wears a bush jacket and disappears off into the sunset. Africa is to be pitied, worshipped or dominated. Whichever angle you take, be sure to leave the strong impression that without your intervention and your important book, Africa is doomed.[37]

Indeed, as I contemplated the ways in which images of women caring and shopping were integral to doing good in the world, it seemed that the earlier moments at the beginning of the century of learning to love Africa showed how caring became necessary to the North's relationship with Africa. I briefly summarize this work to unpack how powerful this moment was in making possible contemporary entanglements between caring for Africa and being a good American.

## Lesson 1 – Love Africa

Climbing up a small hill, a small group of *Survivor Africa* contestants survey the land that they have been struggling to 'survive', but above it they marvel at its beauty. ('We in Africa'; 2:40:10–2:40:44). The show stranded its participants in the middle of the Shaba reserve, a Kenyan game park, but never names these places; they are simply in Africa. One reward creates a movie theater experience under the stars so the players and us the viewers can watch the Karen Blixen fantasy *Out of Africa* ('Out of Africa'; 4:19:16–4:22:39). This is almost entirely (despite the presence of Robert Redford's character) a romance between Karen Blixen and her Africa. At the reunion show the contestants all mention how much they love Africa, never talking about Kenya, the Shaba reserve, the Samburu people who they met or any specific town through which they traveled. The original act of non-naming (this is not 'Survivor Shaba' or 'Survivor Kenya', just 'Africa') allowed for a devotion to the land to emerge among the contestants, a love affair flourishes with unspecified 'Africa' lending them a backdrop for the discovery of themselves.[38]

## Lesson 2 – Love America

But to turn love into caring action, Lesson 2 required learning to be grateful to be American. Two contestants win the opportunity of taking a goat to a local village ('Village Visit'; 3:15:25–3:25:10). They bump along a road to then drag a goat to – shock – the butcher. In a not yet super familiar scene, they play soccer with the kids (Ethan, one of the players, is a professional soccer player) and leave a hacky sack behind. They then head to a restaurant, which looks cobbled together for the reality show, although the village itself at least seemed to have existed before the production team. Like all *Survivor* episodes, food is everything and so they gorge on large plates of oily chips (very unAmerican-like fries). Lex laughs when Ethan has to run to the long drop outhouse after eating the unfamiliar grease. Children laugh, too. This sets up the opportunity for Lex and Ethan to talk about how lucky they are to be American. Somehow this idyllic day with commerce, kids at play, all the ladies dressed to the nines and delicious food suggests a society that lacks what Americans have.

## Lesson 3 – Save Africa

In a still unusual gesture for the take-no-prisoners competition show that is *Survivor*, another reward, which also goes to Lex, was to take a supply of medicines to a local clinic. This reward does double duty of advertising the second element of the prize, a Chevy Avalanche SUV/truck hybrid for loading and transporting the supplies and of offering the show a chance to help. There is little explanation for this trip to Wamba hospital – in 2001 the assumption that Africans needed AIDS testing kits was simply a given. This scene at the hospital takes place between two men, the rocker Lex who won the reward and the European doctor who runs the clinic, but it sets up a long-lasting relationship between Africans and Americans, one founded on love and care. While still an exceptional moment in the show's 20 years, it does have long term impact. Not only is a *Survivor* AIDS charity launched at this season's award show, but *Survivor* continues to use its post-show swag sales to raise funds, now for cancer charities, after *Survivor Africa* winner, Ethan Zohn, is diagnosed twice with cancer.

## The Caring White Women Shopper

When clicktivism or slacktivism, like *KONY 2012*, flattens out ambivalence and empties humanitarian spaces of complex critiques, doing good no longer requires actually traveling and no longer needs celebrities.[39] Rather, it thrives on a narrative of care and the translation of caring into consumption by campaigns like (RED) and companies like TOMS shoes and Warby Parker sunglasses. By establishing shopping as caring these brands trade on the assumption that caring has value in a way that helps deny the political and patriarchal gestures of this kind of consumption. They depend on and exploit the 'common sense' idea that caring is feminine and that it is women who control the mall, in real life and in the virtual world.[40]

Ishita Roy's analysis of another reality television show that sends an American family to Kenya, the National Geographic Channel's *Worlds Apart*, makes an explicit link between the good American woman helping Africa and shopping.[41] A family of four, the Palmers from New Jersey are packed off to spend a week with the Orgubas family in a rural Kenyan village. Although the Orgubas are English-speaking Nairobi professionals, this encounter takes place in their family's 'ancestral' village. The usual tropes of encounters between the modern and the primitive ensue: strange food, fetching water from a distance, hard work for mom and sister and lessons on being a good 'man' for dad and brother. The Palmers learn the same important lessons taught by *Survivor*: Kenyans value family just like they do, and they showed them the importance of spending more time together. But women do not have the same opportunities as men, so Kenya has failed as a 'developed' country. This failure is primarily due to their lack of consumer goods, which the United States offers, evidence of its superiority. This is an encounter, Roy argues, more about how a US brand is built and redefining or reminding American viewers what their values are – good American values such as family, community, integrity, balance between work and life and security. More important here, this is achieved primarily by the American mother who is able to buy the commodities that Kenyan women suffer without and thereby show herself to be both free of patriarchy and a good women/mother. Ultimately these television shows construct the reality of how the good American mother needs to save Africans, not only by consuming products themselves but also by making everybody else good consumers of American products.

Much of the contemporary shopping for caring is feminine in its products and its symbols. In a quick perusal of the websites and marketing materials of many BOGO companies, women are front and center as the potential consumers. They are often feminine brands that evoke a woman's role in maternal care. Shoes, eyeglasses and cell phones are perhaps less gendered, but certainly many brands depend on the idea that it is women who are most likely to be caring through consuming. Gendered examples include Vanity Fair bras, Y.O.U. underwear, soaps and body wash from SoapBox and Lunette menstrual cups; when Milford wants women to BOGO, they sell their condoms in candy-like pastel colors. Yet men most certainly create the industry and drive it. TOMS, the most famous of these one-for-one brands, has come under a great deal of critical scrutiny.[42] But men like TOMS' founder Blake Mycoskie and Warby Parker glasses founders, Neil Blumenthal, Andrew Hunt, Jeffrey Raider and David Gilboa have no problem embracing a public space of earnest do-goodness and entrepreneurial savviness.[43]

While broader critiques of global politics and international relations take seriously the work that gender does either in structuring helplessness as especially feminine or saving the world as penetrative and masculine or as mothering and nurturing,[44] much of the critique of the White Savior Industrial Complex via parody or in other forms starkly focuses on women as its representative. Madonna and even Oprah are frequently lambasted for their disingenuous and ignorant attempts to do good on the continent (I have certainly done this). Not always, of course and not exclusively, but enough to suggest one way in which the industry is perpetuated and men still get off (pun intended) is the gendered displacement of blame from men to women. As long as it's about women or femininity, the critique of the WSIC seems less important.

Critiques of the WSIC in other sites also trend to ridicule women. Even in the late 2010s when #oscarsowhite went viral and critiques of white savior films became part of the zeitgeist, the image of the white savior was often a woman. These critiques do important work in highlighting that it isn't just the centrality of Whiteness but the erasure of the work of black filmmakers and other producers in the industry that requires change.[45] Parody and other forms of satirical comedy skewer these tropes in Hollywood films and on television, making fun of the white savior, the magical negro and the ways that black characters in so much media exist entirely to help white characters evolve or become better. Very much like the role Africa is meant to take in relation to Americans in general. *Hidden Figures* and *Green Book*, with their white male protagonists in stories about black women and a black man respectively, were masterfully satirized on a 2019 skit on *Late Night with Seth Meyer*.[46] Yet Emma Stone in *The Help* and Sandra Bullock in *The Blind Side* are far more likely to be pictured in discussions of white saviors. Despite this critique, *The Help* got a huge ratings surge and larger viewership during the summer of 2020 when increasingly visible violence against black Americans rocked the country, pointing to satires' fine line between love and hate.

The White Savior Industrial Complex in the 21st century, founded as it is on shopping and consuming, is gendered in similarly complex ways to other mediated and bodily ways of engaging with Africa. Such mediated form of travel to Africa was prescient of many of the characteristics of the contemporary extractive politics of care. The images that most frequently circulate for creating this kind of caring consumption are often rooted in the classic gendered tropes of what it means to be a good woman. This is one reason I have returned to my work with Laura Hubbard that shows how the 'adventurer' is constituted as the gesture of the conqueror and its attending act of love in the contemporary. Love of the land and submission to its emptied vistas is no longer enough – both an ethic of care and a relocation of experience from the gaze to the body are demanded of the neoliberal adventurer.

This feminizing and thus domestication of the critiques against saving Africa is also visible in earlier narratives of caring for, or engaging with, Africa. Initially disregarded as frivolous and trivial, the women who undertook adventures during colonial times and wrote to tell about them were portrayed as the queers and eccentrics of their period.[47] The cross-dressing Isabelle Eberhardt, for example, traveling through North Africa as a Muslim man in the late nineteenth century is a complex, orientalist and colonial figure. Her practices ran counter to many colonial ideologies[48] as she pushed the boundaries of self and other, colonized and colonizer. Mary Louise Pratt's reading of Mary Kingsley, who wrote about her travels to Sierra Leone and Angola in the late 19th century, argues that instead of the master-of-all-I-survey sensibility, Kingsley uses humor and comic irreverence to trace her experiences across the continent.[49] These strategies are not unlike the many voluntourists who use parody to circumvent the problems they know full well exists with the ways they are traveling and helping. But as Pratt argues, though Kingsley took a stand against domination, her writing ultimately supported European expansion. Not surprisingly, the most common representations of voluntourists are young white women.[50] While such women's narratives and bodies complicate an easy gendering of the adventurer and colonial domination, they remain complicit and within the love story of self-encounter enabled by the positioning of Africa within the WSIC.

Adventure tourism mimics sex tourism in its penetration and its essentially male action.[51] In my essay with Laura Hubbard on adventure travel in the edited volume *Tarzan was an Ecotourist,* we were interested in the national anxieties between Africa (although a continent) and the United States that are played out through adventure travel and adventurous travel. In looking closely at the ways travelers represented and talked about their adventures in Africa we explored the possibility that the phallic penetration of Africa occurs boldly/bodily through 'doing Africa' and that both male and female adventurers are able to achieve this. As with sex tourism, adventure tourism does not simply gaze on but offers opportunities for penetration. Women who have sex while on holiday see themselves, and are perceived as, engaged in romance tourism rather than sex tourism. This so-called 'Shirley Valentine syndrome', after the 1989 film that sent an English woman to Greece to get her groove back, suggests that western women can head south and have sex with Caribbean or African men in order to invest their own lives with meaning prohibited by the gender roles they are forced to play back home.[52] Development workers, especially in sub-Saharan Africa experience a similar tension between the freedoms women can find in Africa both through the privileges of Whiteness and the out of context-ness of their femininity while they remain subordinate to the masculine development worker.[53]

The White Savior Industrial Complex is at once penetrative and extractive – sending young Westerners into sites of supposed suffering so that they can earn moral, professional and sentimental capital. Such penetration and extraction are characterized by masculine action and language, so it is no surprise that a common criticism of the WSIC is that it constructs a systemic way for white men to appear to save brown and black women from brown and black men.[54] The entrepreneurs who make it possible for western men and women to shop for a cause remain masculine figures, if only in their ability to control their narratives and their origin stories. Women, like their 19th century contemporaries, disturb this landscape of control only to render it palatable for men to conquer. The United States manifest destiny is barely disrupted here; in fact, it is resuscitated in the pioneering spirit of shopping to save the world.

Yes, there are changes to styles of representation, and parodic critiques suggest everybody understands the issues. But in finding a comfort zone in shopping for good, consumption becomes just another form of capitalizing the work of philanthropy and disguising the causes of inequality. It reveals how much the ways Americans engage with Africa follow the trajectory of the United States' own socio-political state. More importantly, it speaks to the strength of a foundational myth about America – its intrinsic superior mores that are best disseminated through consumption. I would suggest that much like colonial and contemporary iterations of Euro-Americans engaging with Africa, the queering of this encounter, or feminizing of it, does not rewrite the narrative of dispossession but contributes to undermining its critique. Consumption builds on and redefines the gendering of care as women's work and fits snuggly into neoliberal economic and social institutions with nary a friction. So, a new figure emerges, the shopper, once again disembodied within the relationship, but continuing to structure the savior as outside of the problem. Yet she remains the embodiment of it, within her role in the form of digital purchasing. The moral economy of the shopping-to-donate equation produces a particular kind of politics that is not simply the individualizing anti-politics of neoliberalism but a social politics of care that thrives in a neoliberal economy.[55] It is made possible by making women the best people to act out in this economy but also perpetrator of all that is wrong with it.

There is a remarkable consistency over the last two decades in how Africa is represented and framed as space that needs saving, and yet, it exists in the face of a multiplicity of funny satirical challenges to the idea of Westerners going to Africa to save it that appeared in the interim. In the next chapter, I explore the ultimate White Woman Consumer who has translated her iconic femininity into a critique of the white savior. The satirical Instagram account Barbie Savior shows how critiques of imagining Africa as a place that needs help and constructing that help in the spaces of consumption and social media can hide the extent to which the white savior narrative mobilizes and depend on massive corporate and government investment, programming, manufacturing and branding. This critical media space continues to support and generate a good American citizen as consumer who is still the same adventurous participant in the quest to save Africans. The surprising similarities between the journeys of young Americans at the turn of the century and their seemingly much more critical and politicized contemporaries 20 years later help to expose the paradox.

## Notes

1. Mathers, Kathryn. 2010. *Travel, Humanitarianism and Becoming American in Africa*. New York: Palgrave.
2. Drawing on Nelson Goodman's idea of worldmaking, Gürsel's observations of photo editors at the beginning of the War on Terror offers a glimpse into the ways that images make the world we live in and do not just represent it. See Gürsel, Zeynep Devrim. 2016. *Image Brokers: Visualizing World News in the Age of Digital Circulation*. Berkeley: University of California Press, Hall, Stuart. 1997. *Representation: Cultural Representations and Signifying Practices*. London: Sage Publications Ltd, Kleinman, Arthur and Joan Kleinman. 1996. 'The Appeal of Experience; the Dismay of Images: Cultural Appropriations of Suffering in Our Times.' *Daedalus*, 125: 1–23, Sontag, Susan. 1977. *On Photography*. New York: Picador USA and Sontag, Susan. 2004. *Regarding the Pain of Others*. New York: Picador USA.
3. See Cole, Teju. 2012. 'The White-savior Industrial Complex.' *The Atlantic*, March 21, developed after his tweets went viral.
4. This reflection on KONY2012's 10th anniversary, describes slacktivism's impact: Emma Madden, Emma. 2022. 'KONY2012: 10 Years Later.' *The New York Times*, March 8, 2022. www.nytimes.com/2022/03/08/style/kony-2012-invisible-children.html.
5. See 'Oprah and Bono Shop (RED).' October 13, 2006. www.oprah.com/style/oprah-and-bono-shop-red/all.
6. Olwig, Mette Fog, ed. 2021. 'Introduction: Commodifying Humanitarian Sentiments? The Black Box of the For-profit and Non-profit Partnership.' *World Development*, 145(September), Richey, Lisa Ann, Hawkins, Roberta and Michael K. Goodman. 2021. 'Why Are Humanitarian Sentiments Profitable and What Does This Mean for Global Development?' *World Development*, 145. Richey, Lisa Ann and Stefano Ponte. 2011. *Brand Aid: Shopping Well to Save the World*. Minneapolis: University of Minnesota Press.
7. Kahn, Carrie. 2014. 'As "Voluntourism" Explodes in Popularity, Who's It Helping Most?' *Goats and Soda: NPR*, July 31, 2014. www.npr.org/sections/goatsandsoda/2014/07/31/336600290/as-volunteerism-explodes-in-popularity-whos-it-helping-most.

8. These figures are reviewed in Mostafanezhad, Mary. 2014. 'Volunteer Tourism and the Popular Humanitarian Gaze.' *Geoforum*, 54: 111–118 and McGehee, Nancy Gard. 2014. 'Volunteer Tourism: Evolution, Issues and Futures.' *Journal of Sustainable Tourism*, 22(6): 847–854.
9. See Kushner, Jacob. 2016. 'The Voluntourists Dilemma.' *The New York Times Magazine*, March 22. www.nytimes.com/2016/03/22/magazine/the-voluntourists-dilemma.html?_r=0.
10. Center for Responsible Travel's Trends and Statistics Page from 2019. www.responsibletravel.org/wp-content/uploads/sites/213/2021/03/trends-and-statistics-2019.pdf.
11. See for example: Achebe, Chinua. 1999. *Hopes and Impediments: Selected Essays*. New York: Penguin Books, Castillo, Susan and David Seed. 2009. *American Travel and Empire*. Chicago: Liverpool University Press, Cooper, Brenda. 2002. *Weary Sons of Conrad: White Fiction Against the Grain of Africa's Dark Heart*. New York: Peter Lang Publishing Inc, Duncan, James and Derek Gregory. 1999. *Writes of Passage: Reading Travel Writing*. London and New York: Routledge, Pratt, Mary Louise. 1985. 'Scratches on the Face of the Country; or, What Mr Barrow Saw in the Land of the Bushmen.' *Critical Inquiry*, 12: 119–143, Pratt, Mary Louise. 1992. *Imperial Eyes: Travel Writing and Transculturation*. London and New York: Routledge, Thiong'o, Ngũgĩwa. 1986. *Decolonising the Mind: the Politics of Language in African Literature*. Heinemann Educational.
12. See Beckles, Hilary and Verene A. Shepherd. 2007. *Saving Souls: The Struggle to End the Transatlantic Trade in Africans*. Kingston, Jamaica and Miami: Ian Randle Publishers, Bell, Morag. 2000. 'American Philanthropy, the Carnegie Corporation and Poverty in South Africa.' *Journal of Southern African Studies*, 26(3): 481–504, Hall, Bruce S., Shah, Ami V. and Edward R. Carr. 2014. 'Bono, Band-Aid, and Before: Celebrity Humanitarianism, Music and the Objects of its Action.' In *Soundscapes of Wellbeing in Popular Music*, ed. Paul Kingsbury, Gavin J. Andrews and Robin Kearns, 269–288. Burlington, VT: Ashgate, Mathers, Kathryn. 2013. *Shared Journey: The Rockefeller Foundation, Human Capital and Development in Africa*. New York: The Rockefeller Foundation.
13. See for example: Mather, K. 2012. 'Mr Kristof I Presume: Saving Africa in the Footsteps of Nicholas Kristof.' *Transition 107*. W.E.B. Du Bois Institute for African and African American Research, Mathers, K. 2018. 'How to Not Photograph Nigerian Women . . . Again.' *Africa is a Country*, May 16, 2018, Mathers, K. 2014. 'Op-Ed: Why Won't White Savior Complex Go Away? Western Aid to Africa is Just Neocolonialism in Sheep's Clothing.' *Take Part*, July 23, 2014.
14. See our website here: www.whenisayafrica.com/.
15. The literature from both volunteers and scholars is exploding, for example: Biddle, Pippa. 2021. *Ours to Explore: Privilege, Power, and the Paradox of Voluntourism*. Lincoln, NE: Potomac Books, Henry, Jacob. 2021. 'The Spatial Imaginaries of International Volunteer Teachers: Contrapuntal and Disconnected Geographies.' *Education, Citizenship and Social Justice*, 17(2): 171–187 and 2020. Whiteness in transit: the racialized geographies of international volunteering, *Social & Cultural Geography*, 21(Dec 11): 1–17, Ji Hoon, Park. 2018. 'Cultural Implications of International Volunteer Tourism: US Students' Experiences in Cameroon.' *Tourism Geographies*, 20(1): 144–162, Sin, H. L. and S. He.

2019. 'Voluntouring on Facebook and Instagram: Photography and Social Media in Constructing the "Third World" Experience.' *Tourist Studies*, 19(2): 215–237.
16. See Kaylan Schwarz' rich ethnographic work with 27 British undergraduates who volunteered in Kenya: Schwarz, Kaylan C. 2017. 'Volunteer Tourism and the Intratourist Gaze.' *Tourism Recreation Research*, 43(2): 186–196, Schwarz, Kaylan C. 2016. *"It's Not Voluntourism": Unpacking Young People's Narrative Claims to Authenticity and Differentiation in the International Volunteer Experience*. Unpublished PhD Dissertation, University of Cambridge.
17. The NGO Global Exchange, especially made sure to educate participants on correct photographic behavior, now reframed as socially responsible travel at https://globalexchange.org/2017/07/31/what-is-socially-responsible-travel/.
18. Ntarangwi, M. 2000. 'Education, Tourism, or Just a Visit to the Wild.' *African Issues*, XXVIII: 54–60.
19. Gunnarsdottir, Elsa Lilja. 2016. *Volunteering in the Neoliberal Subjectivity: Repackaging Problematic Narratives of the Past*. Unpublished Honors Dissertation, Duke University and Schwarz, Kaylan C. 2017. Ibid.
20. Cheung Judge, Ruth. 2021. 'Refusing Reform, Reworking Pity, or Reinforcing Privilege? The Multivalent Politics of Young People's Fun and Friendship Within a Volunteering Encounter.' *Antipode*: 1–21, Cheung Judge, Ruth. 2016. 'Negotiating Blackness: Young British Volunteers' Embodied Performances of Race as They Travel from Hackney to Zimbabwe.' *Young*, 24(3): 238–254, and Henry, Jacob. 2020. 'Whiteness in Transit: The Racialized Geographies of International Volunteering.' *Social & Cultural Geography*, 21(Dec 11): 1–17.
21. Bornstein, Erica. 2001. 'Child Sponsorship, Evangelism, and Belonging in the Work of World Vision Zimbabwe.' *American Ethnologist*, 28(3): 595–622 and Zarzycka, M. 2016. 'Save the Child: Photographed Faces and Affective Transactions in NGO Child Sponsoring Programs.' *European Journal of Women's Studies*, 23(1): 28–42.
22. Richey, Lisa Ann. 2016. '"Tinder Humanitarians": The Moral Panic Around Representations of Old Relationships in New Media.' *Javnost – The Public*, 23(4): 398–414.
23. Biddle, Pippa. 2014. *The Problem with Little White Girls (and Boys): Why I Stopped Being a Voluntourist*. https://pippabiddle.com/2014/02/18/the-problem-with-little-white-girls-and-boys/.
24. Kascak, Lauren and Sayantani Dasgupta. 2014. 'Voluntourism is Ultimately about the Fulfillment of the Volunteers Themselves, Not Necessarily What They Bring to the Communities they Visit.' *Pacific Standard*, June 19, 2014. https://psmag.com/economics/instagrammingafrica-narcissism-global-voluntourism-83838. In a more recent essay Schwartz and Richey suggest that the satirical representations offer a counter-narrative that helps voluntourists manage their self-representation in what they term anticipated "Digilantism." Schwarz, Kaylan C. and Lisa Ann Richey. 2019. 'Humanitarian Humor, Digilantism, and the Dilemmas of Representing Volunteer Tourism on Social Media.' *New Media & Society*: 1–19.
25. Gunnusdottir. 2016. Ibid and Mathers, Kathryn and Elsa Gunnarsdottir. 2017. '"Doing Good" in an Age of Parody.' *Africa is a Country*, January 1, 2017. https://africasacountry.com/2017/01/doing-good-in-an-age-of-parody.
26. Schwarz, Kaylan C. 2016 and 2017. Ibid.
27. Read about it here; https://dukeengage.duke.edu/.
28. See for example: Sampathkumar, Mythili. 2017. 'Angelina Jolie "Offered to Act as Bait" to Capture African Warlord Joseph Kony.' *The Independent*,

Monday, October 9, 2017. www.independent.co.uk/arts-entertainment/films/news/angelina-jolie-kony-bait-capture-africa-icc-chief-prosecutor-moreno-ocampo-a7991676.html, Flock, Elizabeth. 2012. 'Kony 2012 Campaign Gets Support of Obama, Other.' *The Washington Post*, March 8, 2012. www.washingtonpost.com/blogs/blogpost/post/kony-2012-campaign-gets-support-of-obama-others/2012/03/08/gIQArnHkzR_blog.html.
29. Mansour, Carol. 2006. *Invisible Children*. Invisible Children.
30. Articles like this indicate that the organizations can show very little evidence of how its successful social media and 'hearts and minds' campaigns used its funds in Uganda to benefit the children themselves: Titeca, Kristof and Matthew Sebastian. 2014. 'Why Did Invisible Children Dissolve?' *Washington Post*, December 30, 2014. www.washingtonpost.com/news/monkey-cage/wp/2014/12/30/why-did-invisible-children-dissolve/.
31. Cooper, Helen. 2017. 'A Mission to Capture or Kill Joseph Kony Ends, Without Capturing or Killing.' *New York Times*, May 15, 2017. www.nytimes.com/2017/05/15/world/africa/joseph-kony-mission-ends.html.
32. See for example the viral video by Rosebell Kagumire, Kony. 2012. *My Response to Invisible Children's Campaign*, March 8, 2012. https://rosebellkagumire.com/2012/03/08/kony2012-my-response-to-invisible-childrens-campaign/ and commentary from Angelo Izam at https://angeloizama.com/daniel-comboni-joseph-kony-and-jason-russell-faith-in-change-along-the-nile-valley-kony2012/.
33. See Budabin, Alexandra Cosima. 2019. 'Caffeinated Solutions as Neoliberal Politics: How Celebrities Create and Promote Partnerships for Peace and Development.' *Perspectives in Politics*, 18(1): 60–75, Daley, Patricia. 2013. 'Rescuing African Bodies: Celebrities, Consumerism and Neoliberal Humanitarianism.' *Review of African Political Economy*, 40(137): 375–393, Jefferess, David. 2002. 'For Sale – Peace of Mind: (Neo-) Colonial Discourse and the Commodification of Third World Poverty in World Vision's "Telethons".' *Critical Arts*, 16(1): 1–18, Magubane, Zine. 2008. 'The (Product) Red Man's Burden: Charity, Celebrity, and the Contradictions of Coevalness.' *The Journal of Pan African Studies*, 2(July 24, 2009).
34. I am so appreciative for the discussion on these issues during the 'Caring Through Consumption I: What Is at Stake in Development and Humanitarian Practices?' panel at the International Studies Association Annual Meetings in Toronto, 25–31 March 2019, with Alexandra Budabin, Catia Gregoratti, Natalie Forea Hudson, Lisa Ann Richie, Anika Bergman Rosamond, Kaylin Schwarz and especially Roxani Krystalli for her thoughtful reading of the paper.
35. Hubbard, Laura and Kathryn Mathers. 2004. 'Surviving American Empire in Africa: The Anthropology of Reality Television.' *International Journal of Cultural Studies*, 7: 437–455, Mathers, K. and L. Hubbard. 2006 'Doing Africa: Travelers, Adventurers and American Conquest of Africa.' In *Tarzan Was an Eco-Tourist . . . and Other Tales in the Anthropology of Adventure*, ed. Luis A. Vivanco and Robert J. Gordon, 197–213. New York and Oxford: Berghan Press.
36. See Hubbard and Mathers. 2004. Ibid. for descriptions of popular cultural forays into Africa.
37. Wainaina, Binyavanga. 2005. 'How to Write About Africa.' *Granta*, 92(Winter).
38. Hubbard and Mathers. 2004. Ibid.
39. Madden, Emma, 2022. Ibid.
40. See for example: Cairns, K., J. Johnston and N. MacKendrick. 2013. 'Feeding the "Organic Child": Mothering through Ethical Consumption.' *Journal of*

*Consumer Culture*, 13(2): 97–118, Davidenko, M. 2019. 'Searching for Lost Femininity: Russian Middle-aged Women's Participation in the Post-Soviet Consumer Culture.' *Journal of Consumer Culture*, 19(2): 169–188, Freedberg, Sharon. 1993. 'The Feminine Ethic of Care and the Professionalization of Social Work.' *Social Work*, 38(5): 535–540, Roberts, Mary Louise. 1998. 'Gender Consumption, and Commodity Culture.' *The American Historical Review*, 103(3): 817–844, Štante, Nadja Furlan. 2019. 'The Feminine (He)Art of Caring and the Power of Feminine Divine as New Ethics of Peace and Ecojustice.' *The Ecumenical Review*, 70(4): 651–660.
41. Roy, Ishita Sinha. 2007. 'World Apart: Nation-branding on the National Geographic Channel.' *Media, Culture, and Society*, 29(4): 569–592.
42. Costello, Amy. 2012 *Tiny Spark: TOMS Shoes: Is It Good Aid*? https://nonprofitquarterly.org/toms-shoes/. Accessed March 5, 2012.
43. Even when addressing critiques of these models, their male leaders receive praise, for example: Caplan, Josh. 2014. 'How Toms Shoes and Warby Parker Give Differently.' *TriplePundit*, December 17, 2014. www.triplepundit.com/story/2014/how-toms-shoes-and-warby-parker-give-differently/38481. Tobin, Amy. 2013. 'Social Justice: Toms Shoes – Not the Story You Might Expect.' *ARCOMPANY*, October 13. https://arcompany.co/social-justice-toms-shoes-not-the-story-you-might-expect/.
44. Hodzik, Saida. 2017. *The Twilight of Cutting; African Activism and Life after NGOs*. Berkeley: University of California Press, Rankin, K. N. 2001. 'Governing Development: Neoliberalism, Microcredit, and Rational Economic Woman.' *Economy and Society*, 30(1): 18–37, Sharma, Aradhana. 2008. *Logics of Empowerment: Development, Gender, and Governance in Neoliberal India*. Minneapolis: University of Minnesota Press.
45. *The White Savior Trope, Explained*. The Take, July 1, 2020. www.youtube.com/watch?v=w1vuhrFfEkE.
46. *White Savior: The Movie Trailer*. 2019. Late Night with Seth Meyers. www.youtube.com/watch?v=T_RTnuJvg6U. Accessed February 21, 2019.
47. Mills, Sara. 1991. *Discourses of Difference: An Analysis of Women's Travel Writing and Colonialism*. London: Routledge.
48. Smith, Sidonie. 1995. 'Isabelle Eberhardt Travelling Other/wise: The "European" Subject in "Oriental" Identity.' In *Encountering the Others*, ed. G. Brinker-Gabler. Albany: SUNY.
49. Pratt, Mary Louise. 1992. Ibid.
50. Almela, Marta Salvador and Nuria Abellan Calvet. 2021. 'Volunteer Tourism and Gender: A Feminist Research Agenda.' *Tourism and Hospitality Research*: 1–12.
51. As Mary Louise Pratt argued, "It is hard to think of a trope more decisively gendered than the monarch-of-all-I-survey scene. Explorer-man paints/possesses newly unveiled landscape-woman" (1992: 213. ibid). See also Clark, Steve, ed. 1999. *Travel Writing & Empire: Poscolonial Theory in Transit*. London and New York: Zed Books, Pettman, Jan Jindy. 1997. 'Body Politics: International Sex Tourism.' *Third World Quarterly*, 18(1): 93–108, 101 and Spurr, David. 1993. *The Rhetoric of Empire: Colonial Discourse in Journalism, Travel Writing and Imperial Administration*. Edited by F. Jameson, *Post-Contemporary Interventions*. Durham and London: Duke University Press.
52. Gilbert, Lewis. 1989. *Shirley Valentine*. Panavision, Ltd., Paramount Pictures. The 1998 film *How Stella Got Her Groove Back* (Directed by Kevin Rodney Sullivan) based on the novel by Terry McMillan sends a Black American

woman to Jamaica to make a similar discovery. It is just as implicated in this circuit of imperialist sex tourism as Paulla Ebron shows in her chapter, 'Traffic in Men'. In *Gendered Encounters: Challenging Cultural Boundaries and Social Hierarchies in Africa*, 1997, ed. O. H. Kokole. London: Routledge.
53. Heron, Barbara. 2007. *Desire for Development: Whiteness, Gender, and the Helping Imperative*. Waterloo: Wilfrid Laurier University Press.
54. Mather, Kathryn. 2012. Ibid, fulfilling Gayatri Spivak's critique.
55. Bourdieu, Pierre. 1998. 'The Essence of Neoliberalism.' *Le Monde Diplomatique*, 12.

# 2 The Barbie Paradox – How Parody Is Trying to Save Africa

In a video from Comic Relief's 2007 UK fundraiser, Ricky Gervais visits a village in Kenya and conducts an interview with a bereaved Kenyan in a word-perfect enactment of classic celebrity appeals from Africa.[1] He seems to be strolling through a shanty town or township in a nameless African city and ducks into a corrugated iron lean-to to speak to a man about his brother's death. He is interrupted by writing partner, Stephen Merchant, revealing that he is filming in a studio in front of a green screen. Gervais quickly dismisses Merchant's outrage about how dishonest this is by explaining that this way he can just as easily show how bad things are for 'suffering Africans' without putting himself through the trouble of a long flight and the apparent nastiness of life in 'Africa'. He makes not so subtle references to how this kind of show of caring can reap benefits for promoting his new show; "*Extras* on BBC 2 Sunday nights" – he deadpans for the camera. Merchant quickly jumps on the possibility of raising his profile for film roles – British films he qualifies, as Gervais skeptically widens his eyes to the camera in disbelief at the possibility of Merchant getting a movie role in Hollywood. Soon they reset, and we hear again the story of the Kenyan man's loss as Merchant and Gervais weep in sympathy, especially when he pulls out an old tape cassette of U2's greatest hits album. Jaime Oliver, mocking his persona as healthy eating advocate by gorging on fast food fries and turkey twizzlers, is next to interrupt and asks to participate since, in his words, he hasn't been seen crying on TV for a few days. Sir Bob Geldoff, former front man of the Boomtown Rats and the icon of celebrity humanitarianism and Live AID impresario, interrupts this excess of sentiment, but even his disgust at how immoral it is to fake an appeal is soon overridden by possible benefits for raising money.

Even more paradoxically, the normally deeply earnest Bono pulls off a black man's mask, á la *Mission Impossible* movies, to reveal himself as the Kenyan talking about how U2 helped him get through the loss of his brother. It is hard to imagine this kind of blackface even in the interest of an institution like Comic Relief going unremarked upon now, as it seems to have been then. Another U2 Band member, The Edge, even reveals himself as a local Kenyan woman. Zine Magubane has argued that Bono's desire to save Africans is grounded in a sense of shared experience as a 'black European'.[2] She, however, and hardly controversially, disputes that his identity as a marginalized Irishman successfully creates a coeval space with the Africans he helps. It is possible that this was a moment when white European men were allowed to play black people, but I suspect even Bono might have come under fire for embodying a Black African, though I have not found any reflection of this and the skit remains readily available online. It is shocking that this group of comedians/artists did not even consider that dressing up as Africans might be offensive. Africanness was just another role to play, a punchline for Gervais' satire about famous people doing good.

The early 2000s were characterized by the kind of earnest appeal to young Americans and other Westerners mocked here, asking them to care about Africa and to see themselves, with little irony, as global citizens with the intent, affect and means to change the world. But as I described in Chapter 1, over the two decades since, a circuit between global suffering and frivolous shopping and pop culture produced a now familiar tension between good intentions and good publicity. This often took the form of the fast-growing industry of traveling to do good with its own couple name – voluntourism – and its own visual practices. At the same time an often brilliant and biting push back, frequently in satirical or parody form like Gervais' skit, existed alongside and even within the programs supporting the saviors. The paradox continues to grow as young travelers flock to opportunities to save the world or present themselves on social media as caring global citizens yet simultaneously create and mobilize a critical self-awareness of their actions. In this chapter, I go back over this period to try to understand the paradox that makes it possible for good substantive critiques to be incorporated into media and pop culture while the fundamental ways that Americans tell stories about Africa remain the same. I explore how in the midst of biting parodic critique, both the volunteer travel industry and the sense that young Westerners are the only people who can help Africa continue to flourish in the United States.[3] I show how the entanglement of parody and sentiment exposes the ways that Africa continues to figure so powerfully in the meaning of Americanness and argue that a critique of the white savior is essential to navigating the humanitarianism industry as a good American.

## Celebrity Saviors

Gervais' skewering of celebrity humanitarianism came during a golden age of celebrities saving Africa, often through a heartfelt journey into a landscape of devastating poverty and helpless children or through earnest yet quirky visual campaigns – a period I described in my book on Americans discovering their best selves in Africa.[4] A prime example was Alicia Keys' Keep a Child Alive 2006 campaign – 'I am African'. This profoundly earnest series of images of celebrities, including Alicia Keys, Gwyneth Paltrow, Liz Taylor, Sarah Jessica Parker, Seal and Giselle, photographed in stark black and white, painted over in some kind of allusion to 'tribal' face paint in purples and blues, declare 'I am African' and ask for support to fight HIV/AIDS in Africa. At its core is a primeval claim that we are all from Africa. These images were so silly that it opened the door to the start of conversations about celebrities, social media and doing good, as well as produced a searing parody version. 'I am Gwyneth Paltrow' featured a very generic image of 'African women' and text that reads:

> Help us stop the shameless famewhores from using the suffering of those dying from AIDS in Africa to bolster their pathetic careers now that they are no longer dating Brad Pitt and no one gives a shit about them. Just kiss my Black ass to help.

This particular poster was all over the web at the time, but I was never able to track its origin, even then.[5] Perhaps because the original campaign was designed by Somalian-American supermodel Iman and at the time there was a growing acceptance, celebration, or resignation (depending on who you asked) of data showing an evolutionary and genetic origin for humanity in Africa, critiques tended to focus on specific celebrities whose Whiteness was especially stark, like Paltrow. This moment was at the vanguard of a decade at least of massive pop culture and mediated engagement with saving Africa that created a flourishing representational politics of helping and launched an equally pervasive culture of satirical critique.

The persistence of sentimental celebrity appeals in the face of critiques exploded in 2014 when Band Aid 30 gathered a group of original and new pop stars to sing a rewritten version of the 1984 song 'Do They Know It's Christmas' to raise funds for the Ebola epidemic striking Liberia, Guinea and Sierra Leone. Rock star and activist Bob Geldof was joined by Coldplay, One Direction, Ed Sheeran and other stars from the original and those better known to a younger audience to sing a tone-deaf lament about African suffering.[6] Not surprisingly, this raised the hackles of many Africans who used social media platforms to push back against the demeaning lyrics and the ways the whole project silenced the work done by local doctors, nurses and health departments in West Africa.[7] African musicians, including Ivorian reggae star Tiken Jah Fakoly, Mali's afro-pop singer Salif Keïta and Senegalese rapper Didier Awadi had even produced their own fundraising music video – 'Africa Stop Ebola'/*Africa Contre Ebola*. But as Liberian writer and scholar Robtel Pailey defiantly declared on a BBC news show, Geldof made no effort to promote the work of these musicians or of local health care workers.[8] Instead, Band Aid 30 earnestly sang what were frankly ludicrous words about reaching out and touching Africa.[9]

## Seeing the Problem

Yet when Band Aid 30 was released, the landscape of pop culture's celebration of helping Africa seemed to have shifted from the self-aggrandizing moment of a Cloony or Angelina or a *KONY 2012*. Social media platforms created instant global sharing opportunities for travelers as well as the locals they were visiting, and earnestness evolved into awareness of the problems of western aid in Africa. As the second decade of the millennium began, my students at Duke arrived in my classes increasingly self-conscious of the critiques circulating about their desire to go abroad to help. It seemed that everybody understood there was a problem with the ways Africans had been used in these campaigns, and they knew they should think twice about how to talk about their volunteerism or activism and especially how to represent their presence in helping. Teju Cole's seven infamous tweets on the White Savior Industrial Complex, developed into an article for *The Atlantic*,[10] spoke directly to their sense of disquiet about their actions, even calling out *KONY 2012*: "6- Feverish worry over that awful African warlord. But close to 1.5 million Iraqis died from an American war of choice. Worry about that". But it was only one of the voices raised against the uncritical celebration of white saviorism.

Students were well aware from classes, blogs and other online sources, as well as their own research or discussions in high school, of a wide range of scholarship critiquing aid and humanitarian intervention.[11] The Human Sciences Research Council (HSRC) in South Africa wrote an impactful report on orphan tourism showing how voluntourism is one of the drivers of family break up in very poor countries by incentivizing orphanages to run as businesses.[12] Post 2009 they had all listened to Chimamanda Ngozi Adichie's TEDGlobal talk on 'The Danger of a Single Story'.[13] Online projects such as #endhumanitarindouchery made clear the problems of voluntourism in a language understood by the aspiring voluntourists.[14] They devised a list of the seven sins of humanitarian douchery that volunteers should avoid.[15] These were: Research Slothery (lack of research on volunteer organizations and host communities); Workin' Pride, which gets in the way of the realization that they might not be suited (or qualified) for certain types of work; Volunteering as Gluttonous Consumption (treating their trip like any other act of consumption); Greedy Grabby Volunteering, which is blinded by a 'me me me' attitude that leads them to impose their values on the host communities they visit; Fishing for Envy (making themselves look good and making others jealous; Lusting for Likes by flaunting their experiences on social media and, last but not least, Ragingly Enlightened Wrath or looking down on others for not having done the same thing.

## Earnest Responses

The astute and funny critiques do seem to have had some impact on the ways fundraising agencies and voluntourists are portraying suffering in Africa. By the late 2010s, both agencies and individuals adjusted, at least in the ways that they portrayed their work. By 2019 even UK Labour MP David Lammy got the memo and accused Comic Relief UK of white saviorism in response to their representation of BBC producer and *Come Dancing* champion Stacy Dooley's visit to Uganda.[16] The images that circulated in the press showed Dooley in the classic pose of a young pretty white girl hugging and holding black children. These could be stock images for a multitude of voluntourism agencies and fundraising appeals, and they resemble hundreds of photographs on Tinder and other social profiles. It clearly caused a bad taste in many people's mouths at this particular moment. In 2021, the BBC announced that it would no longer send celebrities to Africa to make fundraising videos.[17] Lammy's critique of the image echoed many conversations about white saviorism and made the essential points that the BBC was not putting Africans themselves at the forefront of appeals for aid, nor was it asking important questions about how and why people needed help in the first place. Dooley's own defense reads almost identically to another journalist, Nikolas Kristoff, who ten years earlier bore some scrutiny for his own insistence on reducing complex problems in places like Africa to simple solutions for white people to solve.[18] Unlike Kristoff, she was being called out at a time when the white savior complex was a meme as well as a hashtag. Things have changed in some ways over the last two decades. In the United States, NBC has partnered with Walgreens to air national Red Nose Day fundraisers since 2015, though it does not have the massive pop culture footprint that the charity has in the UK. While it also sends celebrities to Africa,[19] it focuses increasingly on poverty gaps and literacy programs in the United States.

Organizations like the Global Fund, whose (RED) campaign brought compassionate consumption to the forefront of mediated aid work, stopped showing suffering and hopelessness. Their bloated celebrity laden marketing campaigns and highly criticized expensive bureaucracy[20] has led them to shift their social media presence to reflect a more muted approach. By 2020, their video-based media was making little reference to suffering or to specific spaces or people. They focus on happy smiling people, including celebrities and beneficiaries of their projects, and highlight (RED) products in high-end style.

A short video on their own website illustrates the changes they have been making to their brand. A young woman, Melissa, wanders through recognizable backdrops of a poor 'African village' but is at least telling her own story of struggle to keep up with schoolwork and to stay safe during the COVID pandemic.[21] She is a specific young woman with a name and talks in her own language about her school – Sihlengeni Secondary School in, we discover eventually, Umguza, Zimbabwe. She tells a familiar story about lack of online learning and isolation from teachers and peers. But Melissa also describes trying to sell food to men at a local mine and how "some girls are sexually assaulted". She tells her story against a familiar backdrop of a typical African woman going about her chores. We see Melissa fetching and carrying water on her head, gathering firewood and carrying it on her head past chickens and scrappy kids sitting in the dirt. Melissa's role is to represent the entire sub-Saharan Africa where, the film's text tells us: "adolescent girls and young women are more than twice as likely to acquire HIV than their male peers; COVID-19 threatens to put even more girls at risk. Funds are urgently needed to help countries fight COVID-19".

(RED), even as it changes, here resorts to tired and familiar tropes. It is true that young girls in Zimbabwe and elsewhere on the continent are experiencing particular struggles as a result of COVID. But challenges like missing school and patriarchal violence are much more contingent on specific place, nation or community while at the same time not specifically 'African'. (RED)'s tagline is 'UNITE to FIGHT', but it seems that they missed an opportunity here to show how young people all over the world are struggling with surprisingly similar challenges.

Many of (RED)'s videos focus on the products, the sexiness of being a change-maker and music video style montages of artists and activists. The short video '(RED) Revolution 2020' explains how it all works in short texts in a music video showing brand names, earnest people, artists and celebrities doing things (RED) all over the world. On the surface, this might seem like an improvement at first, but when these narratives attempt to describe what the messages mean and what the organizations are working for, they falter. Images of black nurses and black mothers and children who could be anywhere but are portrayed in standard fundraising appeals mode in sites that look like the hospitals or schools visited by fundraisers in the past run alongside the campaign messages on the screen: "(100%) Goes to Fight AIDS". Ultimately these appeals still trade on an unspoken assumption about who needs the funds raised as the helplessness of Africans remains clear. It leaves out the fly infested baby or the boys and girls scrabbling for food on a waste dump but shows the people and sites helping them, representing need in much more subtle but recognizable ways.[22] As always, such appeals leave out any conversation about the structures and causes of global inequality.[23] The organization is still grounded in unchanging ways Westerners' want to understand their space in the world – as the people who save others who need them.

So, though some changes have been made, as producers are being increasingly careful and thoughtful about how they represent Africans, representational strategies continue to depict a particular politics of care and saviorism that seem unchanged and that leaves out structural analysis while voluntourism continues to grow.[24] It seems that the parodic critiques of both the representations and the relationships that led to these changes, that I explore in more detail in the next sections, have done little to shift these politics and might even help support the system.

## Satirical Challenges

The satirical newspaper, *The Onion*, published a short piece in 2014 entitled '6-Day Visit to Rural African Village Completely Changes Woman's Facebook Profile Picture'.[25] The title alone mocks the classic go-to-Africa-and-change-your-life trope. The piece describes a young white woman just returned from volunteering in a Malawian village, declaring: "As soon as I walked into that dusty, remote town and the smiling children started coming up to me, I just knew my Facebook profile photo would change forever". The online zine *Reductress*[26] also wrote a satirical piece in 2014 about taking photographs with kids. It describes "the four cutest ways to photograph yourself hugging third-world children". These lessons were learned from Oprah and Angelina, who the piece describes as understanding that giving should never just be for the sake of giving. The photo-op is essential "so your hope and goodwill have lasting effects, at least on social media". The tips presented reproduce the classics of humanitarian imagery such as cradling the child to your bosom, playing football (soccer) with all the village children, wearing traditional native garb to emphasize your reverence for this alien culture and the essential family portrait of you crouching down with your host family. The tone is clear in the piece, but even as I describe it here it is hard to convey just how to tell the difference between this kind of satirical piece and the many sincere guides on how to take ethical photographs.[27]

In 2016, 'Millennials of New York' – a social media based send up of 'Humans of New York' – produced a well-conceived and effective parody of taking profile pictures. The short video is filmed with pitch perfect earnestness and seeming news-doccy seriousness.[28] Sonya comes to a studio recommended by her friend to pose in front of a green screen with polystyrene balls so her pictures can be photoshopped with young Africans or

Peruvians. She chooses the latter since "Ghana washes her out". US-based critiques of the white savior like this are not limited to Africa but understand, perhaps, that America's 'white man's burden' began in the Philippines and extends across the 'Global South'. Once Sonya's image is loaded, there is a moment of (gasp) go for it as she posts her picture. The photographer waxes lyrical about what a great feeling it is to help people get their perfect profile pic and talks about other clichéd social media situations he produces, including the always classic 'cut off hot chick' – a photo of the subject with a seemingly beautiful woman cut out of the image he posts.

The Tumblr account 'Humanitarians on Tinder' launched early 2014 (now also on Facebook and Instagram) has produced its own publishing subgenre and simply curates images from the dating or hook-up app Tinder.[29] Tinder allows potential dates to quickly scroll through photos of possible partners and decide with a swipe left or right if they would like to connect. The parody site, 'Humanitarians on Tinder', exploits the multiple photos showing (mostly white) participants holding, hugging, lifting up or posing alongside young Black or Brown visibly impoverished children. These images were (and remain) the quickest shorthand for demonstrating virtue, thus attracting positive responses (a right swipe).[30] Many of these postings are of Europeans, but the joke crisscrosses the Atlantic and illustrates the global forms of both saving Africa and critiquing these gestures at the same time. This Tumblr is largely a shaming site – 'oh look at how whities make themselves sexually attractive'. 'Humanitarians on Tinder' is still active on Facebook with new submissions coming in, though these are uncurated in the sense that they include images from all over Instagram and other social media sites. It remains unclear in recent posts whether the interlocutors understand the satirical intent.

#endhumanitarindouchery who offered earnest guidelines for being a better humanitarian also made satirical videos, like *If Voluntourists Talked About North America*, in 2015. Here a young white man asks how he can help "the youths of North America". He wonders if he could teach Zumba to help the "obesity problem"; he tries to raise money through a lemonade stand, guilting people about not caring about "the youths of North America" or "being the change" and celebrating his "optional excursion to Walmarts" to interact with real North Americans.[31] The WordPress blog 'DEAR TOTO[32]' illustrates a similar critique with images of young black kids playing with white kids by carrying them around on their backs as if they were the horses and the white kids were horse riders. One caption reads: "Look, Mom! They can carry the white man, and I can carry the white man's burden!" The Tumblr 'Gurl Goes to Africa' makes an especial point of roasting images of white travelers with black (read African) children. 'Gurl Goes to Africa' launched in January 2014 with this headline: "I went to Africa and all I got was these pictures". Its description summarizes the tone of so much social media around 2012–2016:

> You go to one of those fabulously elitist schools where everyone talks about privilege, classism, racism, sexism, etc. as if they don't practice it in real life. But in order to really see the world, they decide to go somewhere where they can understand what their privilege looks like. So they choose AFRICA! Yay! A whole continent dedicated to helping white people understand what it means to be poor and undeveloped.
>
> This is for all you fabulous biddies who decided that Africa was the right place for you. There's nothing like good 'ole exotification to fill up your time while basking in the hot Saharan sun, wearing your "traditional" African clothes, eating "weird" foods and taking as many photos of black children as possible. You go, Gurl with lots of privilege! This is dedicated to you.

These sites were not alone, but they gained some attention on different media platforms and represent the kinds of parody produced by observers of white saviorism.

## When Agencies Parody Agencies

In a priceless example of parodic critique and earnest do-goodness made by Europeans in English but thoroughly enjoyed in the United States, UNICEF Sweden made a series of short videos in 2013. Jesus, Ghandi and Mother Teresa are thrown together at dinner with an everyday guy who joins their party by 'clicking a banner', thus buying a gift for Christmas in the interest of saving children's lives.[33] *The Dinner Party – The Good Guys Christmas* opens in a formal dining room complete with a chandelier, crystal glasses filled with red wine and dark paneled bookshelves and side boards and large chimney place. Mother Teresa is telling Ghandi that it was so nice of him to starve himself for the sake of the people. A character clearly meant to be (white) Jesus reassures her "you are not so bad yourself Teresa; you spent half your life working for the poor". Teresa declares she just did what anybody would do but that he sacrificed himself for mankind. "Yeah well", Jesus shrugs and turns to say, "Hey new guy, how did you get here?" We see a youngish white dude on his phone who sheepishly says "I just clicked a banner" – "Great job", they all say as they toast him.

The next entry in the video sequence – *Jesus Goes Online* – opens with the words: "Meanwhile at the House of Goodness".[34] The same anonymous

Every-Guy' shows Jesus the internet and demonstrates how to move the cursor to the banner and click. Jesus is excited to try, but clicks the wrong banner, opening a body-building site. Ghandi and Teresa come and have a look and, though Teresa is not interested in trying, Ghandi is thrilled. When he succeeds, they all congratulate him on saving lives by clicking on the banner. The third chapter – *The Greatest Story*[35] – begins as Jesus finishes reading the bible and concludes saying, "there you are, that's my story". Teresa declares "you have done so many good things", and Ghandi muses about what a great story Jesus tells. Every-Guy shakes his head saying, "and so long". "Too kind", says Jesus and turns to Every-Guy, saying "tell us everything" as he pours water into a glass, which turns into wine. The same anonymous white guy describes how he grew up in a suburb as a middle child, which was hard, finished school and went to Australia. "Volunteering, I suppose", says Ghandi. "No, just partying and surfing", Every-Guy responds. He goes on to describe how he returned home and was looking for a job and one day he saw a banner from UNICEF that said it could change lives and clicked it and here he is. "It's like your whole life led you to this moment", says Teresa. Every-Guy deprecatingly says, "oh, I must be a late bloomer". And Jesus reassures Every-Guy that though he is a late bloomer, when he bloomed, he blossomed. It seems clear that we are meant to understand how ridiculous it is to compare the schlubby everyman who has never done anything interesting with philanthropic all-stars like Mother Teresa and Ghandi. Yet it is deadly serious that clicking an online banner will save lives, using the tag line "Doing Good Has Never Been So Easy", seemingly without irony.

Let's look at another series of videos enthusiastically promoted by my students – NORAID's Radiators for Norway campaign.[36] This super earnest appeal is all about changing stereotypes and was inspired by Anja Bakken Riise' experiences in Durban, South Africa as a Development Studies graduate student from Oslo, Norway.[37] Riise describes in her TEDex talk how her professor at the University of KwaZulu-Natal in Durban, who she calls her guide to all things African, asked her whether it would be okay to represent Norway the way Africa is often represented. This revelatory question inspired her as a member of, and later president of, SAIH (The Norwegian Students' and Academics' Assistance Fund) to launch Radi-Aid to try to challenge these images. Radi-Aid produced the viral and admittedly fabulous music video mocking the sentimental and heart-strings pulling of the original Band Aid mega-selling single, 'Do they Know It's Christmas', and the USA version, 'We are the World', that sought to raise funds for Ethiopian famine relief in 1984.[38] Radi-Aid's music video, *Africa for Norway*, came out in 2012 after the 'We are the World 25' remake for Haiti in 2010 and before Band Aid-30's revival of 'Do they Know It's Christmas' for Ebola in 2014.

The video begins with a shocking exposé of the ways Norwegians are suffering from the cold, and an appeal to Africans to send radiators (space heaters) to Norway to help them. The appeal segues into musicians arriving to a studio mimicking the arrival of Geldof, Bono and others for the Band Aid video. The song then does a pitch perfect rendition of the kind of sentimental ballads about Africans, recognizable from 'We are the World' and Band Aid, this time featuring poor freezing cold Norwegians. As time passed and the originals became less familiar to a new generation, I had to first show my students the 1980s videos so they would get the joke.

This initial campaign video *Africa for Norway* quickly received over 2 million views on YouTube, tens of thousands of shares on Facebook and worldwide media coverage. It was so popular that Radi-Aid made another one for Christmas that parodies classic humanitarian fundraising tropes in a story of a suffering family in Norway.[39] In this version, a young African man speaks sentimentally about the suffering of Norwegians using the kind of odd details evoked in generic appeals – like the father, a truck driver, who is away; the whinny dog seen through a frosted-up window; a mother holding her sad-looking children closely by a fireplace all with a weeping violin background. These details have nothing to do with the causes of poverty or marginalization but echo the ways classic appeals from World Vision, for example, focus on seemingly personal details of a child needing sponsorship. The spokesperson peers through the window at this pathetic looking white family explaining that it is not enough to just send warmth, children are catching colds, slipping on ice. The spokesperson explains, again hitting the same kind of cliché that characterizes typical appeals, "Africans need to remember that a white Christmas is also a cold Christmas; give a girl a match she will be warm for 5 minutes; give a girl a radiator she will be warm the whole winter".[40]

The next viral NORAID video in 2014 skewered the growing voluntourism industry in a segment called *Who Wants to be a Volunteer*. This mashes up a number of reality competition shows, including *The Apprentice*, the *Amazing Race* and especially *Who Wants to be a Millionaire?* It focuses on Lilly, a young white woman who wants to win the chance to save Africa. It opens with highlight of her journey in (imaginary) earlier episodes. So we see Lilly completing challenges like the Feed Africa challenge where contestants run around a city throwing bags of flour (at least that is what it looks like) at people on the street who look bewildered; the Educate Africa challenge where an outdoor school is used to teach football moves, and Lilly shows African children how to safely cross a street in the middle of a very rural looking village; the Promote Africa challenge shows the contestant taking photos of herself feeding a baby goat and setting up a Facebook page. The video then goes 'live' where we see her in the final round trying to answer one question to win the chance to save Africa (the grand prize) in a rendition of the *Who Wants to be a Millionaire?* set. The question posed with deathly seriousness is: "How many countries are there in Africa?" The multiple-choice answers were:

A: One; B: Two; C: Five; D: Fifty

"Oh boy, this is a tough one", Lilly says. "I should know this one." She decides to use one of her lifelines – call a friend. The host says "well, you have helped them so much . . . let's see if they can help you". They call a young 'African' child, Michael, who is thrilled to hear from his friend Vusi (the host). Lilly starts reading the question but the screen on the Skype call freezes, and when Michael comes back they don't get the question out before time is out. "Damn African line speeds", exclaims the host.

So, she has to guess – hmmm, deep breath, "A: One"
"Final Answer?" "Yes."

After a long pause, the host declares, "Well Lilly, looks like you going to have to pack your bags (another pause), but you not going home, you are going to have to save Africa".
"That's amazing!" says Lilly.
"Hurry, Africa is not going to save itself!" he shouts, and everybody breaks into dance including some dancers dressed in what looks like traditional (reminding me, at least, of Zulu cultural village) style. The song itself seems to either be forgetting the critique the video is making or is meant to be satirical, as it sings about hearts beating like a jungle drum among other stereotypes. On the screen over this performance are NORAID's taglines.

Stereotypes Harm Dignity
Challenge the Perceptions
Volunteer Now at Rusty Radiator Awards

NORAID has followed up the success of these parodies with other comic takes on the landscape of giving. In 2013 they offered a behind-the-scenes take on Michael, the humanitarian appeal actor, where a young boy bemoans the challenges of acting as a poor dispossessed African for charity appeals while teaching a celebrity how to cry appropriately on camera. The Radi-App, launched in November 2016, allows a do-gooder to give the gift of giving – "Change a life with one swipe". In 2019, Africa Corps Radi-Aid 2.0 made fun of corporate social responsibility. These all skirt the fine line of good satire and could easily pass as 'real' appeals.

## Caring White Woman Shopping

Another site for parodic critique is the viral Instagram account for Barbie Savior, @barbiesavior, launched March 2016, that brilliantly critiques the trope of the white savior.[41] It perfectly renders the tensions between criticizing representational tropes about African neediness, shopping for good and satirizing one's own doing-good impulses. Barbie here stands in for all those women who care too much and try to do good by shopping and giving and volunteering.

Barbie Savior inserts Barbie dolls and her friends in classic scenes of Westerners in Africa along with astute and biting captions. For example, Barbie stands in front of a worn-out chalkboard saying "Who needs a formal education to teach in Africa? Not me", while extolling the value of optimism and highlighting it all with the hashtag #theyteachmemorethanIteachthem. Another image plays on the volunteer with children trope as Barbie feeds a doll cola and explains how this is the happiest possible moment for this child. Barbie Savior makes full use of the #angelhair, citing Louise Linton's own description of herself as a "skinny white muzungu with long angel hair" in her deservedly maligned book, *One Girl's Perilous Journey to the Heart of Africa*. The account is funny as well as smart, and no classic trope of travel to Africa or of the White Savior Industrial Complex escapes its mocking gaze.

Barbie Savior is fully conscious of Binyavanga Wainana's satirical warning that:

> Readers will be put off if you don't mention the light in Africa. And sunsets, the African sunset is a must. It is always big and red. There is always a big sky. Wide empty spaces and game are critical – Africa is the Land of Wide Empty Spaces.

It gives us the classic image of an acacia tree in front of a sunset remarking: "'The two most important days of your life are the day you were born, and the day you find that perfect acacia tree.'-Mark Twain". This succinctly mocks the tendency on social media to attribute multiple apocryphal *bon mots* to figures like Mark Twain.

The account frequently lambasts photographs of foreigners kissing babies as in one post: "Orphans take the BEST pictures! So.Cute."

In another post Barbie hangs a framed outline of Africa on which is written: "We are Africans not because we are born in Africa but because Africa is born in us", reproducing the archetypal idea of Africa as a single homogeneous space that belongs to everybody except people who live in it. Another post declares:

> The people living in the country of Africa are some of the MOST beautiful humans I have ever laid eyes on. I feel so insignificant next to my new friend Promise. She has no running water, no makeup, no clothes but the ones she herself has sewn, and no strict diet to follow – her figure is kept flawless because she is in a constant state of malnutrition. She has nothing, but she still has raw beauty and Jesus – and now me!

Their use of hashtags is masterly and include many versions of what can be found on multiple earnest accounts such as #blessed, #oneheart, #called and #strangers2secondsago. But strewn among the earnest righteous declarations and tone-deaf nonsense are expressions that make the site's intentions clear. For example, #povertyporn, #notazoo, #youwillalwaysbeacountrytome and of course #whitesaviorcomplex. This account, like NORAID, is pitch perfect in its rendition of a stereotypical young woman heading to 'Africa' to save it while making sure she looks fabulous doing it, but what work does it do in disrupting this very journey for many Americans? Its biting parody of the White Savior Industrial Complex reveals most clearly some of the paradoxes of parodic critiques. As with shopping for good brands described in Chapter 1, the nice white lady is more often than not both the problem and the solution.

## When Africans Enter

One of the goals of my film in post-production – *When I Say Africa* – with filmmaker Cassandra Herrman, examines whether it is possible to produce an alternative set of images. This film tries to understand why even in shared spaces like classrooms and online forums, stories that make Africans the backdrop to American saviors who stay center stage persist. One element of our work is showing the extent to which Africans are increasingly present in these virtual spaces, often ahead of their northern contemporaries, and are masters of Twitter, Instagram, Snapchat, WhatsApp and WeChat, among others I am sure I have not heard about. Ironically, Twitter announced in April 2021 that they were setting up an office on the continent in a statement that read as if Twitter was some kind of global equity project[42]:

> Twitter's mission is to serve the public conversation, and it's essential, for the world and for Twitter, to increase the number of people who feel comfortable participating in it. To do this, we need to make it easier for everyone to join in and provide more relevant experiences for people across the world.
>
> Today, in line with our growth strategy, we're excited to announce that we are now actively building a team in Ghana. To truly serve the

public conversation, we must be more immersed in the rich and vibrant communities that drive the conversations taking place every day across the African continent.

Yet social media sites like Twitter have already been frequently mobilized against the more egregious examples of white saviorism in Africa. For example, in 2012 Ugandan Blogger Rosebell Kagumire spoke out against *KONY 2012*[43] in a video on YouTube with a thoughtful and heartfelt plea to consider Joseph Kony in the broader context of Ugandan and regional history and geopolitics. Her plea has been viewed in various iterations by over 800,000 people. In 2016, Zambians explosively responded to the ludicrous publication of *In Congo's Shadow*, written by Louise Linton, supposedly about her horrific experience of the war in the Congo during her stay in Zambia. Zambians made #LintonLies a trending tweet.[44]

While there are exciting and important spaces for Africans to have their say in virtual medias, it is not clear that this is an arena in which Africans can counter the western imaginary of Africa. As Sean Jacobs suggests, we should be especially wary of celebrating the African voices that are increasingly present in social media.[45] Where does their authority lie, he asks – in simply being 'authentically' African? Beyond the risk of tokenism, especially in the uneven terrain of digital social spaces, the people going to do good in Africa are not just entangled with a critique of this very gesture. They are equally entangled in the same mediated spaces as the people they are supposed to save. The very presence in these shared spaces of commentary by young and digitally comfortable Africans helps to maintain the fiction that the white savior complex is not so bad after all.

## Parody's Limits

Political satire, comedy and carnival have often been sources of radical critique and sites for reversing hegemonic discourse. Comedy and ironic parody have observably contributed to social justice or built critical spaces of intervention in the world of humanitarianism, and increasingly, voluntourism.[46] Parody, however, also risks providing a kind of comfort food version of political critique. A rich scholarship makes clear that when humor and parody is politically radical it is often in a world where there are multiple forms of political engagement and critique.[47] In this world, satire is just one way that socially engaged people can learn about and express opinions about politics and society. But when critiquing or resisting the good intentions of Americans wanting to help Africans, it does seem that such parody becomes the *only* way to expose the problematic assumptions and political ideals and relationships that underlie their stories about *doing good*.

Back in 2010, when I first read Boyer and Yurchak's comparison of American political satire in shows like *The Colbert Report* with parody in late-Soviet socialism, I expected them to predict the fall of the United States empire.[48] It seemed both shocking and yet not at all surprising that political critique in the United States in the first decade of the millennium should resonate so much with political critique in the Soviet Union just before its collapse, when it was in fact dangerous to criticize the state. Boyer and Yurchak call this *stiob*, a form of political parody that "required such a degree of *over-identification* with the object, person, or idea at which [it] was directed that it was often impossible to tell whether it was a form of sincere support, subtle ridicule, or a peculiar mixture of the two".[49] Forms of parody, like *stiob*, are so hyper-identified with the dominant political language and representations because these are so powerful that opposition becomes unspeakable. This is the parodic hypernormalization they see in 'The Yes Men' or *The Colbert Report*. This satire may actually make the world we live in seem ridiculous enough that we do see ways to speak and act outside of it, and that can create a disenchantment with inequalities that otherwise seem natural. But these same kinds of hypernormalizations also suggests a failure to find a language to disrupt hegemonic power. Six years after this essay was published, parody and governance in the United States crashed into each other in the person of the 41st president, and while it might seem that the world collapsed, it in fact went on pretty much as usual for many Americans anyway. I suggest that similarly the parodies of systems of extractive and racist humanitarian practices and discourse described here are less radical than sustaining, allowing us to exist within a social order that we know is wrong.

I am most interested in the ways that Barbie Savior's makers and the people who share her posts and chuckle over them are not outside the industry but have experience or plan to have experience volunteering and, though very much self-aware, are probably also consuming models for better voluntourism. Many of these sites circulate as Gervais' video does within the actual world of aid and philanthropy. UNICEF laughs at the guy who just clicks a banner to become a good guy but is earnest in declaring that "doing good has never been so easy". The site #endhumanitariandouchery, whose seven sins of humanitarian douchery I described earlier also provided visitors to their site (which no longer exists) a responsible volunteering toolkit. This suggested strategies for avoiding the seven sins of humanitarian douchery. They also offered an alternative to this White Savior Industrial Complex – Fair Trade Learning (FTL). FTL has a healthy presence online and describes itself as a

> [G]lobal educational partnership exchange that prioritizes reciprocity in relationships through cooperative, cross-cultural participation

in learning, service, and civil society efforts. It foregrounds the goals of economic equity, equal partnership, mutual learning, cooperative and positive social change, transparency, and sustainability. Fair Trade Learning explicitly engages the global civil society role of educational exchange in fostering a more just, equitable, and sustainable world.[50]

Here is the re-inscription of the Humanitarian Industrial Complex as if it could exist outside of white saviorism.

NORAID might use the Rusty Radiator Awards to select the most egregious use of sentiment for charity fundraising,[51] but they fund and are funded by the Norwegian Students and Academics International Assistance Fund. Sometimes their own supporters get confused. In comments on *Who Wants to be a Volunteer*:[52]

> Geraldine: "You are right. This is a wonderful parody of the 'White Savior Mentality' that permeates so much voluntourism. So much voluntourism today does focus on glorifying the volunteer and making the beneficiaries seem helpless. But BeachCorps is trying to change that. BeachCorps is a model 9 years in the making that focuses on great causes, not the egos of volunteers. After years of developing our model, we were delighted to learn of the seminal work 'Toxic Charity' that talks about the dangers of good intentions doing harm through volunteer work. We talk a lot about Toxic Charity on our website. www.beachcorps.com/avoiding-toxic-charity.html. So ultimately while we believe a lot of voluntourism is bad, not all of it is. We subscribe to the #MendNotEnd philosophy that says you can indeed go good on short term trips if the focus is the cause, not the ego of the volunteer. We hope that folks will see if we are keeping our promises!"

I am forcibly reminded of how Binyavanga Wainaina would tell us about his frustration at responses to his satirical essay on 'How to Write About Africa'. He describes his anger, in a follow up essay to the original, at how readers would send him countless book manuscripts that followed exactly his satirical guidelines for how to write about Africa.[53] Clearly not understanding his parodic and critical voice.

The creators of @BarbieSavior even worked with Radi-Aids SAIH Norway to make a how-to-take-responsible-photographs video called *How To Get More Likes On Social Media*.[54] It uses a series of unfortunate selfie set-ups taken by a visitor to 'Africa' to say that while photographing suffering gets a lot of likes, it is a form of stereotyping. It is similar to @BarbieSavior in its use of hashtags and a comic book figure posing for photos designed to illicit likes. Starting with seeing too little response to her posts, a young woman finds the answer: "Travel to Africa". Once there she follows the signs to 'Real Africa' and finds a stereotypical African village with stereotypical suffering kids and poses to follow the next rule, which is focusing on what matters, her and her caring, strong glutes, etc. Keeping in mind the third rule, "Kids = Likes" and fourth, "Suffering will give you twice the likes", she stops health care professionals from doing their job, posing to take selfies with a kid in hospital. The final rule of course is: "Always remember hashtags", like #getinvolved and #children. These scrolling hashtags go to another one, NORAIDS' #stereotypesharmdignity. This video was especially popular among my students although I struggled to understand just what the message was. Its rules for getting likes are exactly the same as actual advice to improve your social media presence and the satire is meant to be visually obvious, but these gestures are not that obvious, to me anyway.

Stuart Hall warned us that this was inevitable – changing stereotypes without changing the structural inequalities that make those stereotypes damaging has never undermined any forms of bigotry.[55] If the satirists and the aid agencies are so embroiled with each other, what work does parodic critique do within extractive and silencing politics of representation? The very existence of satirical memes that are meant to function as scathing critique render actual critique impossible. What matters here, however, is not whether laughter and parody can somehow displace the inequality in the relationship between do-gooders and Africa or be replaced with 'better' images. The popular culture and media I have described in this chapter that sustain an industry just for white saviors, much like their sentimental versions 15–20 years ago, are merely symptoms of the relationship between Americans and Africa that says a great deal about the United States and nothing about Africa.

While Barbie Savior uses humor to critique relations of domination, she then returns us to where we started. Stephen Wearing *et al.* offer insight into what is left out of critiques of voluntourism that focus on a single and highly gendered and consumerist figure like Barbie as the embodiment of white savior complex.[56] This, they suggest, obscures the neocolonial, neoliberal and consumerists aspects of this industry, as well as possible ways in which voluntourists can work outside of these relations. As the parodies described above show the people who are mocked are elite whites, almost always girls and though they understand they are privileged, they need to confirm its boundaries by going to Africa. This resonates profoundly in the ways that mediated sites of doing good ultimately define privilege and the relationship between 'America' and Africa. But the success of parody to both critique and sustain these unequal relationships is made possible, I suggest, by a very familiar kind of entanglement that has sustained extractive colonial relationships between Africa and the West for centuries.

## Colonial/Postcolonial Entanglements

In trying to think about the ways in which contradictory and in some ways unequal discourses can bump up against each other within a single hegemonic set of rules, which sustains the way Americanness engages with the world, I found myself thinking back to a classic scene in southern African anthropology. In *The Bridge: Notes on a Social Situation in Zululand*, Max Gluckman writes closely and densely about the interactions of actors at a bridge opening ceremony in Zululand.[57] With a penchant for detail, Gluckman first describes the event and all present at a bridge opening ceremony in a way that spatializes the relationships of the people there. He asks where certain actors are located, who built the bridge, who will use it, what kind of ceremony is possible, and even whether there are several 'ceremonies' occurring within the one. This description shifts anthropological focus from the supposed 'customary celebration' to the opening of a bridge, and it just begins to hint at the multiple alliances of each individual and their conflicting interests. The opening ceremony included the European administrators slaughtering a cow and pouring the 'gall' over the bridge to ceremoniously open it from near the banquet table, while the 'Zulus' present removed their hats for the speeches and hymns as they celebrated from the banks of the river. From this bridge opening Gluckman draws the conclusion that the social structures of late colonial South Africa are dominated by processes of economic integration into the broader industrial and agricultural complex that was becoming South Africa. Ronald Frankenberg's reading of this piece, alongside later work by Gluckman, suggests that the important point here was that the schisms between whites and blacks were not evidence of the fact that the two inhabited separate spheres but that they integrated Zulus and colonists into a single system.[58] While showing how black and white inhabited overlapping and mutually dependent, though extremely unequal, spaces, Gluckman was clear that Zulu and settlers were entangled in an established system of White supremacy that in no way supported harmony or true collaboration.[59]

In a much later moment in African history Achille Mbembe describes moments when officials – soldiers, district commissioners, lawyers, policemen – interact, often violently, with citizens of Cameroon to show the banality of power in the postcolony back, I suggest, on the bridge.[60] Public ceremonies, such as executions, medal ceremonies, state visits, funerals and even road blocks designed explicitly to bring together those in power with their subjects, make visible both the logics of the postcolony but also how its operation made common sense. Mbembe shows the ways that politics and power in the postcolony are not quite business as usual, not simply a mimicry of colonial relations of power that required control of bodies in the interest of labor and productivity. Rather, political institutions in the postcolony force participation in their own ceremonies where they can perform an imagined legitimacy that controls bodies. As on the bridge, the ceremonies and rituals of the *commadement* performed as both acts of violence and inclusion do double duty of distancing and domesticating the ruler and the ruled. Mbembe shows how the everyday requirement to participate in ceremonies of power from obeying a border post to dancing at a political rally entangles those in power with those they subjugate.[61]

Parody is both a powerful critique and yet one that silences critical process because it is so successful at creating a shared space between action and critique of that action, allowing the similar coexistence of two seemingly disparate political stances within the same action. Although Chris Rojek suggests that the idea of equivalencies between celebrity humanitarians and ordinary people is "beyond parody",[62] the carefully curated self-representations of young voluntourists discussed in Chapter 1 suggest that their evocation of parody and humor is meant to create the possibilities of just such shared spaces – everybody working together to solve the same problems, aware of the ironies of their engagements. I suggest that parody itself plays a fundamental role in producing this paradox. Parodic critique of humanitarianism in Africa shows that it is the very entanglement between Americans and the idea of Africa that parody allows that produces a false sense of sharing space with each other. This entitles Americans to continue to patronize and exploit Africa.

The overidentification produced by their entanglement in the very structures and institutions they are critiquing gives young Americans a sense of being outside of the problem, because they are aware of the problem. This is an illusion that domesticates all forms of critical questioning. Even while they are fully aware of the inequalities that characterize their relationships with the people they are trying to help and are even informed of the structural, political and social mechanisms by which those inequalities are created, they are, to paraphrase Mbembe, so entangled that they are powerless to do anything but make it ridiculous. Yet in being caught in the same systems of relations on the bridge, parodic critique isn't just a compromised form of activism or an ethically challenging space of critique but a gesture that actively recreates the relations of power.

## The Activist

If there was any doubt that we live in a world in which reality and parody cannot be distinguished or that Americans' ideas about helping and themselves have not changed much in the last 20 years, the reality competition show announced in late summer 2021, *The Activist* (CBS), is a slap in the face of any doubters.[63] It described itself as: "Six inspiring activists work with three high-profile public figures to bring meaningful change to one of three vitally important world causes: health, education and environment". Hosted by Usher (American musician), Pryanka Chopra (Indian actress) and Juliann Hough (American dancer and actor), it was meant to pit activists against each other in competitions to highlight the activists' individual causes. It was produced by music production company Live Nation and Global Citizen, an organization that appears to mobilize celebrity for doing good. Global Citizen funds high-end fundraising social media campaigns including a live concert to raise money and to encourage something they call action. The millions of actions in their name that they claim are helping to end poverty seem to be either donating, possibly reading or learning about an issue or/and retweeting and sharing the organizations' posts.[64] They seem extremely successful at raising money and appear stuck in (what should be but is not) anachronistic dependence on clicktivism and awareness raising. They host the same celebrity driven high-profile events as in the 1980s and their founder and CEO, Hugh Evans, tells the same story young travelers told at the beginning of the millennium – how travel and the encounter with others changed his life as his bio on the organization's website illustrates:

> Hugh is an internationally renowned development advocate and humanitarian. His passion for poverty eradication was sparked at the age of 14 while on a World Vision trip to the Philippines. The abject poverty Hugh was exposed to led him to begin his work challenging the status quo of extreme poverty. Following a trip to South Africa in 2002 as World Vision's inaugural Youth Ambassador, Hugh co-founded the Oaktree Foundation.

It is not surprising that there was a massive push back against *The Activist*, primarily because of its competition aspect and the cheapening of 'real' activism. Global Citizen posted an apologetic tweet that focused primarily on the competitive nature of the show. The producers have been penitent and reformulated the show to leave out the competition and make it more of a 'documentary'.

## Whiteness Winning

The worlds of white savior parodies and anti-black violence collided in this wannabe reality television show that wanted to turn all activism into an absurdist comedy of white saviorism. These absurdist politics are visible in White America's decision to respond to the murder of George Floyd by rewatching *The Help*.⁶⁵ Amanda Hess argues that this is the same satirical algorithm that produces a thriving market on Etsy, Redbubble or even Amazon for T-shirts, throw pillows or socks with George Floyd's face on them, turning tribute into brand. Just another chapter, argues Maya Philips, in the long history of turning Blackness into a commodity beginning with slavery in the United States.⁶⁶ Here, I suggest, lies the power of the paradox I have described in this book, how critique of White supremacy collapses into consumption and satire that only serves to support the system and to reinscribe Africa as belonging to America.

Whiteness is central to this failure of either a satirical gaze or of African voices to disrupt the exploitative and damaging impacts of media grounded in helping or saving Africans. The 'nice white lady' described in Chapter 1, when combined with the satire of nice white lady as *Barbie Savior*, makes apparent how this gesture obscures important elements of the politics of Westerners trying to save Africa – why Teju Cole's insistence of a White Savior *Industrial* Complex remains so salient (my emphasis). But I want to reiterate that these parodic critiques are even more than obscuring. In centering caring white women as the problem, the important points Cole makes especially in calling this out as an industry is lost. Parodic Whiteness is personal not systemic and saving Africa is conveniently separated from systematic racism in the United States. It does similar work as the foregrounding of white fragility and the critique of white privilege in 2020 that is so important for the United States by placing the burden of White supremacy on nasty white women. Parodying 'Karen' abroad turns the gaze away from entanglement between US global hegemony and the American savior who then is allowed to continue acting on behalf of Africans with impunity and celebrated zeal.

The extent to which *The Activist* felt like a parody and a horror story all in in one, so real it is unreal, is made powerfully clear in this comment from a possible contestant, Clover Hogan, a 22-year-old climate activist and founder of youth advocacy organization Force of Nature⁶⁷:

> I remember thinking I was in a *Black Mirror* episode.⁶⁸ When the call ended, I cried and called my mum. The whole time, I was made to feel as if I was failing a test.

*The Activist* shows that horror might be a mediated form of critique capable of disturbing the entanglements between privilege and criticism. Jordan Peel's smash 2017 film, *Get Out*, sent a young Black man into the white wealthy suburban home of his girlfriend's family, where the whites are super friendly but deadly and the Black people – friends and servants – are just plain strange.⁶⁹ *Get Out* is not a funny film about white people; it is funny, but it is first a HORROR film, and second a horror film, not about white people, but about White privilege That is, about the structural forces rooted in Whiteness that oppress black Americans in their own country. As Maya Philips argues in 'The Many Faces of George Floyd':

> Some of this work is trying to capture the surrealism of racism that Jordan Peele invented for *Get Out*. But while that movie introduced to popular culture a critique of white covetousness of Black personhood, it was also about the fear of the loss of oneself, about the plunge into a "sunken place" that results in racial lobotomy. The scares are external. More crucially, they're existential.[70]

In an essay by Malawian scholar Priscilla Takondwa Semphere in the *Huff-Post*, 'Blacker Than You', she reflects on film performances and the success of Black actors from outside the United States instigated by a comment from Black American actor, Samuel L. Jackson. He was referring to award winning British actor Danial Kaluuya's performance in *Get Out*, declaring that a 'brother' (meaning a Black American) would have best played the role.[71] He is channeling larger debates among Black Americans about representation and appropriations. Zakiya Dalila Harris' social comedy about book publishing in the United States, *The Other Black Girl*, for example, articulates this frustration with how white-centered industries circumvent their responsibility to genuinely build equitable work and creative spaces in the United States by pointing to this love affair or greater comfort with a foreign Blackness:

> Yes, we just published 'that Black writer' last year, but that writer, along with the last six Black people we've published here at Wagner, was not a Black American, he was from an African country, and while that's definitely an example of diversity, it's also really not.[72]

It is especially powerful to think about how *The Other Black Girl*, like *Get Out*, becomes essentially a horror story.

*Get Out* shows how racism is not that thing that other people (not us) express through acts of physical or verbal violence but integral to the everyday ways that white people move through and live in the world. It is not a parody of white suburbia; it is a horror movie, making clear that black people's experience of living in America is defined structurally by violence of all kinds. This is not about Barbie going to Africa to save it but about White/American privilege as the infrastructure on which our lives and relations are built. Chapter 3 explores how this privilege becomes apparent in American popular culture meant to create positive representations of Blackness that replicates white savior narratives in their representation of Africa. It reveals

## The Barbie Paradox – Trying to Save Africa    65

the ways colonialism is not in the before/past of the postcolony but is entirely present and articulates relations of the past with those in the present.

## Notes

1. BBC One – Comic Relief – Ricky Gervais, March 22, 2007. www.youtube.com/watch?v=5DgIRjecItw.
2. Magubane, Zine. 2008. 'The (Product) Red Man's Burden: Charity, Celebrity, and the Contradictions of Coevalness.' *The Journal of Pan African Studies*, 2(July 24, 2009).
3. See for example Illingworth, Sarah. 2016. 'Voluntourism, White Saviors and Advocacy vs. News.' *HuffPost Blog*, August 8, 2016. www.huffingtonpost.com/sarah-illingworth/voluntourism-white-savior_1_b_11554968.html. Accessed August 17, 2017.
4. Mathers, Kathryn. 2010. *Travel, Humanitarianism and Becoming American in Africa*. New York: Palgrave.
5. But it was shared in the Tumblr Africans against appropriation: https://thisisnotafrica.tumblr.com/post/28001392173/text-in-picture-reads-i-am-gwyneth-paltrow-help/amp. See also Mohney, Chris. 2006. 'Gwyneth's African Ad Inspires Imitators.' *Gawker*, August 11, 2006. http://gawker.com/193729/gwyneths-african-ad-inspires-imitators.
6. Dearden, Lizzie. 2014. 'Band Aid 30 Lyrics: Reworked Lyrics for Ebola-themed "Do They Know it's Christmas?" Revealed.' *The Independent*, Saturday, November 15, 2014; 16:33. www.independent.co.uk/arts-entertainment/music/news/band-aid-30-new-lyrics-ebola-themed-do-they-know-it-s-christmas-revealed-9863007.html.
7. See for example: BattaBoxNG. 2014. *Do They Know It's Christmas? Africans Speak Out on Band Aid 30!* November 20, 2014. www.youtube.com/watch?v=mMXfRH7mOio.
8. Robtel Neajai Pailey on Band Aid 30. November 23, 2014. www.youtube.com/watch?v=WUESiW-zdTQ.
9. Miller, Sophie. 2014. 'Are the Band Aid Lyrics Really that Controversial?' *BBC News*, November 24, 2014. www.bbc.com/news/newsbeat-30182195.
10. Cole, Teju. 2012. 'The White-savior Industrial Complex.' *The Atlantic*, March 21 and @tejucole.
11. See for example: de Waal, Alex. 2008. 'The Humanitarian Carnival: A Celebrity Vogue.' World Affairs, 171(2): 43–55, Easterly, William. 2007. *The White Man's Burden: Why the West's Efforts to Aid the Rest Have Done So Much Ill and So Little Good*. Oxford and New York: Penguin Books, Hanlon, Joseph, Barrientos, Armando and David Hulme. 2011. *Just Give Money to the Poor: The Development Revolution from the Global South*. Sterling, Virginia: Kumarian Press and Moyo, Dambisa. 2009. *Dead Aid: Why Aid Is Not Working and How There Is a Better Way for Africa*. New York: Farrar, Straus & Giroux.
12. Richter, Linda M. and Amy Norman. 2010. 'AIDS Orphan Tourism: A Threat to Young Children in Residential Care.' *Vulnerable Children and Youth Studies*, 5(3): 217–229.
13. Adichie, Chimamanda Ngozi. 2009. 'The Dangers of a Single Story.' *TEDGlobal* 2009 | July 2009. www.ted.com/talks/chimamanda_ngozi_adichie_the_danger_of_a_single_story?language=en.

14. Although their satirical video is up on Youtube, the site itself is no longer operational: If Voluntourists Talked About North America. #EndHumanitarianDouchery. April 6, 2015. www.youtube.com/watch?v=_8GZjZTZrWA.
15. Banning-Lover, Rachel. 2015. 'The Seven Sins of Humanitarian Douchery.' *The Guardian UK*, Thursday, April 16, 2015; 04.39 EDT. www.theguardian.com/global-development-professionals-network/2015/apr/16/humanitarian-douchery-volunteering-voluntourism-endhumanitariandouchery.
16. This show was the model for the U.S. show *Dancing with the Stars*; Stacey Dooley Comic Relief documentary pics spark 'white saviour' row. Thursday 28 February 2019 14:03, UK. https://news.sky.com/story/stacey-dooley-comic-relief-documentary-pics-spark-white-saviour-row-11650766 K.
17. Comic Relief will stop sending celebrities to Africa. 28 October 2020 BBC News. www.bbc.com/news/entertainment-arts-54716750.
18. Mather, Kathryn. 2012. 'Mr Kristof I Presume: Saving Africa in the Footsteps of Nicholas Kristof.' *Transition 107*, W.E.B. Du Bois Institute for African and African American Research.
19. See for example: Jack Black meets Felix, a street kid in Uganda | Red Nose Day 2016 May 24, 2017. Milo Ventimiglia's Trip to Kenya UPDATE | Red Nose Day USA Mar 30, 2020. www.youtube.com/watch?v=vbKrBxdTVPo #RedNoseDay.
20. 'Bono's ONE Foundation Under Fire for Giving Little Over 1% of Funds to Charity.' *Daily Mail*, September 23, 2010. www.dailymail.co.uk/news/article-1314543/Bonos-ONE-foundation-giving-tiny-percentage-funds-charity.html.
21. *Melissa: Out of School and at Risk of HIV and Violence During Lockdown.* www.theglobalfund.org/en/specials/2021-01-26-15-years-of-red/. Accessed September 24, 2021.
22. Thanks again to Ami Shah for highlighting this dissonance.
23. (RED) Revolution 2020. www.red.org/how-red-works. Accessed September 24, 2021.
24. For some of the changes and continuities see Gharib, Malaka. 2021. 'The Pandemic Changed the World of "Voluntourism." Some Folks Like the New Way Better.' *Goats and Soda*, NPR. www.npr.org/sections/goatsandsoda/2021/07/15/1009911082/the-pandemic-changed-the-world-of-voluntourism-some-folks-like-the-new-way-bette. Accessed July 15, 20212: 24 PM ET.
25. '6-Day Visit to Rural African Village Completely Changes Woman's Facebook Profile Picture.' *The Onion*, January 28, 2014. www.theonion.com/article/6-day-visit-to-rural-african-village-completely-ch-35083.
26. Sharavsky, Andy. 2014. 'The Four Cutest Ways to Photograph Yourself Hugging Third-World Children.' *Reductress*, 1.1. Living, January 9, 2014. http://bit.ly/1f3ux60.
27. See any number of ethical or socially responsible traveler blogs, for example: www.nationalgeographic.co.uk/travel/2020/01/your-travel-photography-ethical; https://erinoutdoors.com/ethics-of-travel-photography/; www.realitytours.org/about-reality-tours/.
28. 'Watch This Girl Get the Perfect Profile Picture.' *Millennials of New York*, April 13, 2016. www.facebook.com/millennialsofnyc/videos/watch-this-girl-get-the-perfect-profile-picture/1678597962392545/, see also Toole, Connor and Alec Macdonald. 2016. *Millennials of New York*. New York: Gallery Books.
29. http://humanitariansoftinder.com/.

30. Mason, Corinne Lysandra. 2016. 'Tinder and Humanitarian Hook-ups: The Erotics of Social Media Racism.' *Feminist Media Studies*, 16(5): 822–837, Richey, Lisa Ann. 2016. '"Tinder Humanitarians": The Moral Panic Around Representations of Old Relationships in New Media.' *Javnost – The Public*, 23(4): 398–414 and Woods, Orlando and Siew Ying Shee. 2021. '"Doing it for the 'Gram'"? The Representational Politics of Popular Humanitarianism.' *Annals of Tourism Research*, 87, March 2021.
31. #EndHumanitarianDouchery: If Voluntourists Talked About North America, April 6, 2015. www.youtube.com/watch?v=_8GZjZTZrWA.
32. https://deartoto.wordpress.com/2014/01/10/gurl-goes-to-africa/.
33. The Dinner Party – The Good Guys Christmas – Eng – Unicef Sweden, December 11, 2013. www.youtube.com/watch?v=7UIdzSsNbZw.
34. Jesus Goes Online – The Good Guys Christmas – Eng – Unicef Sweden, December 11, 2013. www.youtube.com/watch?v=7C37DX8Do7s.
35. The Greatest Story – The Good Guys Christmas – Eng – Unicef Sweden, December 11, 2013. www.youtube.com/watch?v=TrgcrnraUnM.
36. Who wants to be a volunteer: www.youtube.com/watch?v=ymcflrj_rRc The videos are made by The Norwegian Students' and Academics' International Assistance Fund www.saih.no – With funding from The Norwegian Agency for Development Cooperation (Noraid). Video by NEFDT Films www.nefdt.com/ and iKind Media www.ikindmedia.com.
37. From BandAid to RadiAid, Laughing Our way to Change: Anja Bakken Riise at TEDxMuenster (TEDxMünster), June 16, 2013. www.youtube.com/watch?v=rEI8NzMpnho.
38. Here are the celebrity music videos: Band Aid – Do They Know Its Christmas 1984, November 24, 2011. www.youtube.com/watch?v=bmj7KlIut1w. U.S.A. For Africa – We Are the World 1985. www.youtube.com/watch?v=9AjkUyX0rVw. Band Aid 30 – Do They Know It's Christmas? November 17, 2014. www.youtube.com/watch?v=-w7jyVHocTk. We Are The World 25 For Haiti – Official Video, February 12, 2010. www.youtube.com/watch?v=Glny4jSciVI.
39. Find all their videos here: www.radiaid.com/.
40. In 2011, Trevor Noah did something similar to parody the struggles of middle class white Americans: Trevor Noah – UNICEF Spoof – WROARF Public Service Announcement. www.youtube.com/watch?v=cWlAgPJdHdA, April 21, 2011.
41. www.instagram.com/barbiesavior/.
42. Beykpour, Kayvon and Uche Adegbite. 2021. *Establishing Twitter's Presence in Africa*, Monday, April 12, 2021. https://blog.twitter.com/en_us/topics/company/2021/establishing-twitter-s-presence-in-africa.
43. Rosebell Kagumire, Kony. 2012. *My Response to Invisible Children's Campaign*, March 8, 2012. https://rosebellkagumire.com/2012/03/08/kony2012-my-response-to-invisible-childrens-campaign/.
44. Kuo, Lily. 2016. *Africans Are Outraged by this "White Savior" Memoir by an Actress Who Spent a Gap Year in Zambia*. https://qz.com/africa/723430/africans-are-ridiculing-this-white-savior-memoir-by-an-actress-who-spent-a-gap-year-in-zambia/. Accessed July 5, 2016.
45. Jacobs, Sean. 2003. 'Reading Politics; Reading Media.' In *Shifting Selves: Post-Apartheid Essays on Mass Media, Culture and Identity, Social Identities South Africa*, ed. Herman Waserman and Sean Jacobs. Cape Town: Kwela Books.

46. Brassett, James. 2009. 'British Irony, Global Justice: A Pragmatic Reading of Chris Brown, Banksy and Ricky Gervais.' *Review of International Studies*, 35: 219–245, Cameron, John D. 2015. 'Can Poverty be Funny? The Serious Use of Humour as a Strategy of Public Engagement for Global Justice.' *Third World Quarterly*, 36(2): 274–290, Chouliaraki, Lilie. 2012. 'The Theatricality of Humanitarianism: A Critique of Celebrity Advocacy.' *Communication and Critical/Cultural Studies*, 9(1): 1–21, Clark, Jessie Hanna and Jennifer L. Fluri. 2018. 'Everyday Political Geographies of Humor.' *Political Geography*, 68: 122–124, Feldman, Lauren and Caty Borum Chattoo. 2019. 'Comedy as a Route to Social Change: The Effects of Satire and News on Persuasion about Syrian Refugees.' *Mass Communication and Society*, 22(3): 277–300, Olwig, Mette Fog and Lene Bull Christiansen. 2016. 'Irony and Politically Incorrect Humanitarianism. Danish Celebrity-led Benefit Events.' In *Celebrity Humanitarianism and North-South Relation: Politics, Place and Power*, ed. Lisa Ann Richey, 170–188. London and New York: Routledge and Schwarz, Kaylan C. and Lisa Ann Richey. 2019. 'Humanitarian Humor, Digilantism, and the Dilemmas of Representing Volunteer Tourism on Social Media.' *New Media & Society*: 1–19.
47. Boyer, Dominic. 2013. 'Simply the Best: Parody and Political Sincerity in Iceland.' *American Ethnologist*, 40(2): 276–287, Sastre, Alexandra. 2014. 'The "Guido" Situation: Minstrelsy, Parody, and Ethnic Performance on MTV's Jersey Shore.' *Communication, Culture & Critique*, 7: 356–370.
48. Boyer, Dominic and Alexei Yurchak. 2010. 'American Stiob: Or, What Late-Socialist Aesthetics of Parody Reveal about Contemporary Political Culture in the West.' *Cultural Anthropology*, 25: 179–221 and Colletta, L. 2009. 'Political Satire and Postmodern Irony in the Age of Stephen Colbert and Jon Stewart.' *The Journal of Popular Culture*, 42(5): 856–874.
49. Boyer and Yurchak, 2010: 250. Ibid.
50. See for example: Campus Compact. https://compact.org/ftl/. Accessed October 27, 2014. It has also been described in travel literature: Hartman, E., Paris, C. M. and Blache-Cohen, B. 2014. 'Fair Trade Learning: Ethical Standards for Community-engaged International Volunteer Tourism.' *Tourism and Hospitality Research*, 14(1–2): 108–116.
51. NORAID gives out a "Rusty Radiator Award to the fundraising video with the worst use of stereotypes. This kind of portrayal is not only unfair to the persons portrayed in the campaign, but also hinders long-term development and the fight against poverty. The Golden Radiator Award goes to the fundraising video using creativity and creating engagement. This kind of charity campaign is stepping outside of the common way without using stereotypes." www.rustyradiator.com/.
52. www.youtube.com/watch?v=ymcflrj_rRc Accessed September 12, 2021.
53. Wainaina, Binyavanga. 2010. 'How to Write about Africa II: The Revenge.' *Bidoun*. www.bidoun.org/articles/how-to-write-about-africa-ii.
54. *How to Get More Likes on Social Media*. SAIH Norway, November 7, 2017. www.youtube.com/watch?v=7c9mwY31iMI.
55. Hall, Stuart. 1997. *Representation: Cultural Representations and Signifying Practices*. London: Sage Publications Ltd.
56. Wearing, Stephen, Mostafanezhad, Mary, Nguyen, Nha, Nguyen, Truc Ha Thanh and Matthew McDonald. 2018. 'Poor Children on Tinder' and Their Barbie Saviours: Towards a Feminist Political Economy of Volunteer Tourism.' *Leisure Studies*, 37(5): 500–514.

57. Gluckman, Max. 2002 [1940]. '"The Bridge": Analysis of a Social Situation in Zululand.' In *The Anthropology of Politics: A Reader in Ethnography, Theory, and Critique*, ed. Joan Vincent, 53–57. Malden, MA: Wiley-Blackwell.
58. Frankenberg, Ronald. 2002 [1982]. '"The Bridge" Revisited.' In *The Anthropology of Politics: A Reader in Ethnography, Theory, and Critique*, ed. Joan Vincent, 58–64: 60; and see Nuttall, Sarah. 2009 *Entanglement: Literary and Cultural Reflections on Post-Apartheid*. Johannesburg: Wits University Press for reflections on post-apartheid South Africa.
59. Gluckman, Max, 2002/1940. Ibid.
60. Mbembe, J.-A. 1992. 'Provisional Notes on the Postcolony.' *Africa*, 62(1): 3–37.
61. Mbembe, J.-A. 1992: 29. Ibid.
62. Rojek, Chris. 2013. '"Big Citizen" Celanthropy and Its Discontents.' *International Journal of Cultural Studies*, 17(2): 127–141.
63. See the announcement and some responses here: www.tvinsider.com/show/the-activist/.
64. Live Nation Entertainment, Inc. is an American global entertainment company that was founded in 2010 following the merger of Live Nation and Ticketmaster. The company promotes, operates and manages ticket sales for live entertainment in the United States and internationally. According to their website "Global Citizen is a movement of engaged citizens who are using their collective voice to end extreme poverty by 2030. On our platform, Global Citizens learn about the systemic causes of extreme poverty, take action on those issues, and earn rewards for their actions – as part of a global community committed to lasting change." www.globalcitizen.org/en/.
65. Hess, Amanda. 2021. 'Black Squares, Mass-Produced In '8 Ways a Modern Civil Rights Movement Moved the Culture.' *The New York Times*, March 20, 2021. www.nytimes.com/2021/05/20/arts/george-floyd-death.html?campaign_id=9&emc=edit_nn_20210521&instance_id=31283&nl=the-morning&regi_id=85835802&segment_id=58645&te=1&user_id=1e712cf5d3f8899f110f8a9862d76464t.
66. Philips, Maya. 2021. 'The Many Faces of George Floyd.' In '8 Ways a Modern Civil Rights Movement Moved the Culture.' *The New York Times*, March 20, 2021. www.nytimes.com/2021/05/20/arts/george-floyd-death.html?campaign_id=9&emc=edit_nn_20210521&instance_id=31283&nl=the-morning&regi_id=85835802&segment_id=58645&te=1&user_id=1e712cf5d3f8899f110f8a9862d76464.
67. Sullivan, Becky. 2021. *CBS Backtracks on 'The Activist' After a Backlash, Including From One of Its Hosts*, September 16, 2021. www.npr.org/2021/09/16/1037960999/cbs-backtracks-on-the-activist-after-a-backlash-including-from-one-of-its-hosts.
68. *Black Mirror* is an anthology show grounded in the kind of psychological dysphoria and horror of *Twilight Zone*.
69. dir. Jordon Peele, 2017.
70. Philips, Maya. 2021. Ibid.
71. Semphere, Priscilla Takondwa. 2017. 'Blacker Than You: Daniel Kaluuya, The Place of Race and the Race of Place.' *HuffPost*, March 16, 2017. www.huffpost.com/entry/blacker-than-you-daniel-kaluuya-the-place-of-race_b_58c99be8e4b0e0d348b33ff8.
72. Harris, Zakiya Dalil. 2021. *The Other Black Girl*. New York: Atria Books.

# 3 Becoming American in Wakanda or Black is Queen

> I feel the most profound statement I can make about race is to make Panther so cool he transcends the racial divide here in America. Rather than try and force the readers to identify with a black character, I accepted the fact a great many readers would not be able to overcome the race thing, and withdraw Panther from the reader entirely.[1]

Christopher Priest, the Black comic book writer who revitalized the character of Black Panther in a series of comic books for Marvel Comics in the mid-1990s, reflects here about Black superheroes and comic book fans. Priest's Black Panther series was the primary inspiration for the 2018 film, though the times and the graphic medium make them very different and yet surprisingly similar to the film. I am not trying to set up a comparison or read the graphic novels too closely, but their tone and the motivations driving the film's story arc offer some insights into what Black Panther means today. Not least, this struggle over Blackness in the United States in a story about an African hero.

Over a decade of ever more creative consumer driven ways to save Africa that has shifted from missionary and missionary-like travel to viral online social media campaigns back to traveling to do good as voluntourists and around again to shopping or consuming for good, Africa continues to be treated largely in exactly the same ways. Against this backdrop of a contested, yet thriving, save Africa industry, the United States is also coming to terms (kind of) with its legacies of white supremacy. In some ways these have been very different sites, yet they both help to shape and create narratives of white saviors. So, while white allies fulfill their need to help in the struggles against anti-black violence in the United States, Black Americans turn to Africa to find the heartbeat of what they are fighting and striving for. In the middle then is what I want to understand, what is Americanness when Africa and Africans are imagined as largely decorative backdrops to American struggles?

DOI: 10.4324/9781003223818-4

This chapter explores the meaning of Americanness and the intersections between Americanness, Whiteness and global Blackness. I lean into sites of American imaginings of Africa – *Black Panther* and *Black is King* – that explicitly work to emancipate Blackness and ways of being Black in America. If Americans generally look to imagining Africa as a way to make themselves better American citizens, Black Americans imagine Africa as a way to claim spaces of belonging in the United States.[2] I suggest that these gestures to emancipate representations of Africa show how the White Savior Industrial Complex does not work through or depend only on white subjects. Not only is the White Savior Industrial Complex feminized and entangled in its own critique, thereby escaping any real challenges, as previous chapters showed, it also incorporates *all* Americans in a global system that needs stories from Africa to be silent or invisible.

Pop culture spaces do fundamentally necessary work to tell better and brighter and even radical stories about living and thriving as Black in the United States. While Black Lives Matter and other voices force Americans to face up to their racism, more people of color are finding openings and becoming more visible in pop culture.[3] Not only has the importance of media and cultural production that reflect multiple lives and bodies finally reached into actual production and investment (though not enough, for sure), but there is a measurable difference in roles and, just as important, in behind-the-scenes designers, editors, writers and producers.[4] In thinking through visual culture in the United States that centers and values Black lives through evoking Africa itself, I do not aim to undermine the importance and beauty of these projects. I do suggest that while these sentiments matter both symbolically and for fostering radical political change in the US, they do not just function in a cartographic vacuum that liberates Black Americans.

There is a rich and important history of conversations between African and American activists and intellectuals.[5] The United States' history and geopolitical power, founded on slavery and White supremacy, has made Africa central to conversations and struggles for African diasporic voices, and African genealogies are essential to Blackness in the United States. The current movements against anti-Black violence have found many ways to cross borders, not just across the Atlantic, but to the South as well; though we do not know yet whether a worldwide pandemic has created barriers or knocked them down, there is an increasingly common language of struggle around the world against white supremacy.[6] Despite these heightened conversations and the importance of the parallel long history of shared global diasporic struggles for Black emancipation, there are tensions between US and global struggles. Here, I suggest, that part of thinking about how Africa is represented in the United States is to understand the ways these vocabularies about a global Blackness travel seamlessly or with friction.

I focus almost entirely on two recent moments in the American imagining of Africa to try to reflect on what is at stake when Africa and Africans become a site for making America a better place for all. *Black Panther,* released in 2018 as an installment in the Marvel Studio's Avengers saga, was the first (major Hollywood produced motion picture) with a Black or African superhero. The film was first revealed as an important part of the massive multi film arc of the Avengers beginning (chronologically barring *Captain Marvel*) with *Captain America* and ending at least partly with *Avengers Endgame* in 2019. It is perhaps not surprising that the brackets for this saga are the whitest of white superhero Captain America and a film that ends with Captain America passing his shield to the Falcon, a Black Avenger. The other site is the collected visual work of Beyoncé surrounding the redrawn film of Disney's *The Lion King* that birthed a soundtrack album (*The Gift*), a documentary of the making of the music for the film and a visual album, *Black is King*. This chapter explores the work that these visual stories do, what they tell us about Americanness and the limits and possibilities of a global Black struggle, especially when it fails to decenter the United States and its particular history.

## Black Panther

What struck me early on as *Black Panther* was being teased on entertainment news was the congratulatory conversations about a black actor being hired to play a superhero.[7] Some of this conversation was amazement that this comic book would become part of a massive cinematic juggernaut at all given that it was a series about an African and Black superhero. The expectations for the film echoed the feelings expressed in the 1990s by Priest above, who worried about writing a Black hero for a largely white audience. It is an indictment of the film industry in the United States, which is so grounded in Whiteness that it is surprising or shocking that an African character would be played by or remain a Black character and be played by a Black actor. Despite acknowledging Black Panther's origins and power as rooted in the fictional African country of Wakanda, much of this celebration was about a black superhero, not an African superhero, entering mainstream film.[8] Here I am most interested in the representation of Africa and Africanness in a movie that is most definitely about an American superhero played by an American actor, the late Chadwick Boseman.

### The Film and Its Comic Book Inspiration

When Black Panther was given his own comic series, rescued from the Avenger ensemble in the 1990s, even in the writers' room there was a consensus that he was the most boring Avenger; they felt, however, that there was a way to retell his story.⁹ Christopher Priest, their primary writer, was remarkable not just for taking on this particular hero but because he was one of very few Black American writers in the mainstream comic book genre. In a retrospective of his career as the film was coming out, *Vulture* outlines just how rare his voice was – despite a small and powerful group of Black authors and artists. Priest was the first full-time comic book writer or editor at the so-called 'Big Two' of Marvel or DC.[10] While this made him an inspiration for other Black creatives, white colleagues resented his position, even declaring an African-American conspiracy. Priest responded with a "Marvel White Supremacy Memo" that described the contributions made by all the Black creators he worked with and his awareness of the violence inherent in being a Black creative at the mercy of white readers. He would never really feel at home or gain the respect he had earned in the industry, and despite a storied career writing a range of DC and Marvel superhero comics, he eventually became a preacher. His marginal status defined his career, despite Black Panther's success and despite his commitment to the traditional white audience for this genre. He describes his and his team's responses to the challenges of writing a Black superhero in an essay in the collected Volume I of his series. He saw his work as making those white boys as comfortable as possible. In part, this was because he did not want to be a "Black Writer, writing about Black issues or characters". Priest writes in a 'Wakanda mail' entry in one of the earlier comics:

> Sure it's a double standard: I get to make cracks about racial issues that a white writer would be strung up for. But that's not why I do it. Nobody sat me down and told me to make BLACK PANTHER about race. And it's not.

The 2018 *Black Panther* film is grounded in these comic books from the 1990s that describe how a meteorite containing vibranium hit the area where five 'African tribes' fought over the metal. They were united by the ancestor of T'Challa, the current Black Panther, who was the first to be given the superpowers of the Black Panther by ingesting a tea made from a sacred flower. He used this power to unite all but the mountain Jabari Tribe to form the nation of Wakanda. Wakanda is a kingdom in Central Africa – when drawn on maps by fans it seems to appear somewhere between Burundi, the Congo and maybe Central African Republic, or further west between Chad and Nigeria, though in the film it is squashed between Uganda and Kenya. Some maps cluster Wakanda just north of Zamunda (an equally fictional African nation from Eddie Murphy's *Coming to America*) and Nambia (Trump's invented African country before all African countries were described as shit-holes by the same president).[11] It appears to the wider (fantasy) world as a small rural kingdom with almost no technological development, but that is because the meteorite metal vibranium has allowed this small country to develop such a sophisticated technology that it can shield its cities and wealthy agricultural spaces from satellites and planes. While a stalwart of the Avengers comic books since the early days, film fans of the series meet T'Challa for the first time in *Captain America – Civil War* when his father, the King T'Chaka, is assassinated. Prince T'Challa returns to Wakanda to be crowned as the heir to the throne, but he first must go through a ritual approval from the various tribes who unite under the kingdom's rulers.

After the death of his father in the preceding Marvel Avengers film, *Black Panther* opens as T'Challa returns to Wakanda to claim his throne. All tribes come together for the ceremony to 'choose' the next king. T'Challa is challenged to a fight to the death by M'Baku, the leader of a fifth tribe, the mountain-dwelling Jabari who were never united under Black Panther's rule. Before the fight, T'Challa is stripped of the power of the Black Panther to make it fair. While T'Challa is victorious, he allows the challenger, M'Baku, to live. This ritual is a standout in the film as it highlights the work of costume designers who were justifiably lauded for the exquisite design of these clothes. The five tribes are each given a recognizably African print or beadwork or piercings taken from familiar and not so familiar regions across the continent. These include Zulu and Ndebele beadwork and Lesotho-style blanket-wrapped mountain men. Following his victory, T'Challa is taken to a sacred cave where he once again ingests the flower that conveys power and is buried alive. He visits the ancestral plane where he meets his father, T'Chaka, speaking isiXhosa (South Africa actor, John Kani, plays the late king, so not surprising) and learns about his role and his connection to all the ancestral Black Panthers.

One of the most powerful moments in the film is not in Africa, but in Oakland, when T'Challa was only a child. His uncle, Prince N'Jobu wants to use Wakandan technology to help oppressed people around the world, but the king comes to stop him, killing him while his young son plays basketball outside. This sets in motion future assaults on the kingdom's secrecy from Ulysses Klaue, played as a South African arms dealer by English actor Andy Serkis. Though we do not know this immediately, we next see N'Jobu's son, now called Killmonger after his US military experience in Afghanistan, stealing an artefact containing vibranium from a London museum. Tracking these stolen weapons take T'Challa; his sister Shuri, a tech wizard; Nakia, his on again, off again lover and his personal army/body guards the Amazonian-like Dora Milaje around the world where they also pick up CIA Agent Ross, who is after the same arms supply chains.

Killmonger, however, double crosses Klaue and uses his dead body as a way to enter the kingdom. Here he reveals himself as a Prince of Wakanda

T'Challa's cousin and challenges him for the throne. He vanquishes T'Challa, throwing him over a cliff into a roiling river, and takes over the kingdom. After ingesting the power-giving flowers, he burns them all, but not before the warrior Nakia steals some. Nakia, Shuri, Ross, and T'Challa's mother Ramonda flee to seek the aid of the Jabari and learn that M'Baku's men have found and are caring for the comatose T'Challa. He is restored by the flower and returns to battle Killmonger. This leads to a major showpiece battle in the film as the formerly united Wakandan tribes fight on behalf of Killmonger while others range alongside T'Challa. Here the film is able to showcase the battle between the desire to stay hidden and the struggle to bring Wakandan technology to the world to save it.

T'Challa and his family win this battle, but though T'Challa overcomes Killmonger, he allows him to die with dignity. While Killmonger is the villain, he is also one of the most sympathetic characters in the film and has a major impact on both his cousin and Wakanda. Killmonger's rise to power was made possible in part by some of the tribes' frustration at Wakanda's isolation.[12] W'Kabi, head of the border tribes, even tries to engage with T'Challa about the devastating poverty and technological backwardness in the rest of Africa that Wakanda could easily solve. T'Challa essentially dismisses Africa (all of it outside of Wakanda) as hopeless. But when T'Challa finally settles in as king he opens up the country's technology to the world, or at least to the United Nations. This deadly serious scene could have been played much more ironically as an African country stands up and announces it is going to save the world in a reversal of the white savior gesture, though with identical tone and affect. T'Challa then heads back to Oakland, California, not to helpless Africa. Here he establishes a community center at the site of his uncle's murder. This tether to Oakland and to the ways Black people are oppressed all over the world but especially in the US grounds the film, as I believe it is meant to, in the struggles of Black Americans. But it depends on an invention of Africa as devasted and hopeless as any of the highly criticized and mocked ways the White Savior Industry has produced.

## Zamunda

Black Panther's origin story and the villains are straight out of 'Aaafrica' (the all too familiar stereotypical homogeneous space), as this note in the voice of CIA operative Ross, situating the narrative in *Black Panther* 1998 #1 shows:

> You see, back in Wakanda, things were a little TENSE. The client [T'Challa] had set up a refugee camp in the kingdom's border region

where tribesmen seeking ASYLUM from regional ethnic wards would be SAFE. Safe from their governments – but not from EACH OTHER. They kina brought their war WITH them. The client often found himself interceding in skirmishes between the refugees, which aggravated the Wakandan people that much MORE. See, Wakandans come pretty much in TWO flavors – the CITY DWELLERS and the MARCH TRIBESMEN. They never agreed on ANYTHING – until the client granted asylum to the refugees. So, in REVIEW: the city dwellers hated the tribesmen, the tribesmen hated city dwellers, they both hated the refuees who hated THEM in return, despite the fact Wakadna was clothing and feeding them at the time.[13]

In both the comics and the film Wakanda is a haven of what is clearly understood as modernity, human rights and stable government separate from a continent rife with chaos, warfare, tribal violence and superstition.

Eddie Murphy's smash hit from the 1990s, *Coming to America*, followed up in 2020 by *Coming 2 America*, plays off humor rather than heroism to suggest similarly that Africa can only thrive outside of the structures of western colonialism and imperialism. Here the fictional country is Zamunda, which is also ruled by a king, though with little special powers beyond wealth and self-importance and, according to the fantasy cartographers, linked to Wakanda as its neighbor on the continent. Other similarities are visible not least in the films' success at offering Black audiences alternative representations of Blackness while also appealing to white audiences.

Zamunda is more visible in the second and more recent edition, as in the first it is just the place far away that gives Murphy's prince an opportunity to seem naïve about America and to have power and authority and, therefore, sex appeal, a quality considered exotic among the American Black people he engages with. It might also not be surprising how the two very different films resonate together when considering how rare it is to see films with primarily black casts made in the US that are not white savior films or black suffering stories (these are often the same). The problems with how Africa is represented by Zamunda have come under more scrutiny than Wakanda. In fact, Wakanda's strong female characters and American liberal style politics (though this seems to reside entirely in its humanitarian interventions) are seen as an improvement on the Zamundan 'Big Chief' kind of elements. Despite going to the trouble to invent an uncolonized kingdom, Zamunda recreates an 'Africa' characterized by odd (meant to be amusing) customs like court servants cleaning American visitors.

## *The White Man's Burden*

When he took over writing Black Panther comic books, Priest did not want to write about race because he believed that this would be the death of the comic. He drew on a trope he calls 'Chandler Bing' (from the 1990s sitcom *Friends*), the guy out of place that makes viewers or readers feel okay about their own discomfort, to argue for reintroducing Black Panther through a white man's experiences. So, in the books we see T'Challa almost entirely through the lens of a white CIA agent, Everett K. Ross. For Priest, this did double duty of keeping an American white male audience interested, while also having a white man be the butt of all the jokes. As long as readers were laughing at the white man, who in fact got to actually tell T'Challa's story, they would not assume that the comic was 'about' race. The executives who produced *Coming to America* seem to have the same impetus that Christopher Priest addresses in introducing a bumbling white CIA agent when they asked Murphy to include a white character in the first film. Perhaps the broader audiences for film, as well as Murphey's convictions and clout, made it possible for him to resist this and so make a film entirely about Black people.[14] The revitalized graphic books under the helm of Ta-Nehisi Coates, published first in 2016, do not depend on a white interlocutor like the CIA operative Ross.[15] They are beautiful, avoiding some of the problematic misogynistic and 'tribal Africa' tropes of earlier versions and perhaps inspire the strong female characters in the film. Though I cannot offer a close reading here, Coat's version remains stories of an African superhero for Americans.

This type of character appears in the 2018 *Black Panther* as CIA agent Everett K. Ross, (played by British actor Martin Freeman doing double duty as 'colonizer' on multiple levels perhaps) who gets to experience Wakanda as a hapless white dude. His entry in the film is done slyly, allowing for many gentle pokes about white privilege and white masculinity. He is slightly bungling and the butt of jokes and yet his life is saved by superior Wakandan technology, and he ultimately gets to heroically shoot down the plane trying to escape Wakanda with vibranium weapons. While we no longer watch T'Challa's story through the eyes of this character, he remains a stand-in for white guys who might feel like they don't belong as fans of the film. Ross' relationship to T'Challa and his family in the 2018 film is less obviously neocolonial than in the books and yet in some ways more sinister.

Priest was understandably struggling to navigate the consistent and persistent racism in the industry and beyond. All the comic creators were insistent that fans of the Avengers would turn away if they thought the new series was 'about' race or politics or in fact about Africa or 'the jungle'.[16]

Alongside the white narrator, they therefore chose to place the story line and the character in the Bronx, a Black American neighborhood where it seemed his story would be more relatable to white male readers. But it is these same tropes that animate the 2018 film, though with some changes. The Bronx becomes Oakland, California, in the film.

## Coming From 'Africa Is a Country'

Music producer and writer, Boima Tucker, reflects on the place Wakanda holds in Black Americans' celebration of Africa as he explores the tensions between his Sierra Leonian heritage and his Americanness that he experienced growing up.[17] While he pushes against the way "[t]he Africa of Wakanda resembles more an undifferentiated African stew, its parts floating in the red, black and green universe somewhere between Kwanza and Kente", he also celebrates the possibilities of a film that truly imagines a global community of Blackness. Gabrielle Tesfaye, a US film director who has Ethiopian and Jamaican heritage, reiterates an argument about why Black Americans might be attracted to this idea of Africa as a single space:

> For the black diaspora, Africa becomes just one word for an entire continent. It's important to understand that people who are a part of the history of the transatlantic slave trade don't know where in Africa they are from. And that's why the word Africa is a vague thing for them, because they don't know.[18]

This risks, though, assuming a willfully ignorant audience, in fact flattening out Black America, as well as the complexities of enjoying a film full of entitled, authoritative, powerful, Black people. There has been enough evidence of the harm these stereotypes do, so it is worth asking how a global Blackness in Hollywood cinema seems to require this kind of flattening out. Jelani Cobb's review of *Black Panther*, which he loves, also makes explicit the important work it does in connecting Black Americans to their roots on the continent but more importantly connecting them to Black people in Africa and its diasporic communities.[19] He engages with the film's director Ryan Coogler's own reflections about reclaiming African American's lost sense of Africanness. Cobb argues powerfully for the redemptive possibilities of an invention of Africa that lies not in white imperialists narratives like 'Tarzan' but in the hearts and creativity of Black people. It seems though that there are implications to replacing the ahistorical empty space manifested in the interest of colonialism and imperialism in an equally ahistorical space though imagined as complex and powerful.

South African based scholar, Felix Mutunga argues:

> Black Panther engages with anti-Blackness and at the same time affirms Blackness in the backdrop of white supremacy. It's reception and celebration in Africa, US and globally gestures at its centrality in awakening a certain consciousness in Black publics.[20]

The popularity of the film in Africa does not supersede critiques from the continent. As Ghanaian American Erica Ayisi writes (quoted in Mutunga's piece as well):

> The film connects black Americans to a continent that has been positioned as mysterious, disease-infested and dark to the Western world. Moreover, most African Americans are descendants of the slave trade, whose African heritage, customs and religion were deliberately erased and replaced with a European system created by colonisers. Watching the two worlds marry in Hollywood matrimony is prime black pride.[21]

It is hard to overstate the sense of relief and pride in Blackness that the film evoked in black audiences. It was truly important as a significant celebration and affirmation absent from US pop culture. This celebration (well deserved, though it might be of the way such films connect black Americans to Africa) simply assumes that through such celebration of Americans, global Blackness and especially Africans are equally emancipated.

The idea in some conversations about the film that this is somehow a counternarrative to representations of Africa obscures what it means to imagine an uncolonized Africa as the only way to emancipate Blackness. This is, as political commentator Nanjala Nyabolo writes, a film about America for American audiences.[22] What does it say to Africans that their realities do not matter, and they are nothing given those realities? This was the power of colonialisms itself, now reinterpreted as better for Africa. Wakanda is not disturbing simply because it is invented or imagined – Africa is always imagined, as Cobb points out – but those inventions are violent, and they exist solely for the interests of colonialists and imperialists and now their current version of 'white saviors'. If Wakanda recreates Africa as a space that was never colonized, Beyoncé reimagines it as just as empty until she fills it with her gift.

## Beyoncé – African Goddess

On the evening of February 12th, 2017, American pop artist Beyoncé Knowles-Carter graced the stage of the 59th Grammy Awards in a flowing yellow-gold gown and began a performance of divine motherhood and feminine power through a recognizable imagining of Yoruba Goddesses Yemoja and Oshun.[23] Beyoncé's invocation of Yoruba deities during a performance meant to exhibit ideas of the divine is not unfamiliar. She appears as Yoruba water goddess Oshun on her visual album *Lemonade* in 2016.[24] Her 2017 maternity photographs were also replete with references to Oshun and Yoruba symbolism.[25] It was this moment when an American pop queen started telling a story of Black female power through embodying Goddesses from Africa that inspired me to try to understand the similarities between Wakanda and Beyoncé's work for Disney on the *Lion King* film and related visual album, *Black is King*.[26] Beyoncé reiterates her connections to the Yoruba Goddesses explicitly in her first collaboration with Childish Gambino for *Black is King*. In 'Mood 4 Eva' (Beyoncé, Jay-Z and Childish Gambino), she calls herself out as, not just Beyoncé Giselle Knowles-Carter, but as Nala, Oshun and Queen Sheba.

## The Gift

In *Making the Gift*,[27] a companion documentary film to her *Lion King*[28] soundtrack, *The Gift*, Beyoncé lands in a place she calls Africa where she feels at peace because of, she explains, its rhythms and vibrations. The film, directed and produced by Beyoncé, introduces her *Lion King* soundtrack, which would also become the visual album *Black is King*. It meshes James Earl Jones' narration with scenes from the film, combined with standard behind-the-music scenes of artists at work and snippets of the music videos.

In the documentary Beyoncé describes the origin story for *The Gift* in terms of her desire to create a soundtrack that celebrates Africans and African Americans in a way that the whole family can enjoy. She also wished to reclaim South African Solomon Ntsele's (Linda) song 'Mbube', better known as 'The Lion Sleeps Tonight' from Disney's exploitation.[29] Her goal, at least according to her sister, was to give the song its due, apparently ignoring the long legal battle by Ntsele's family against Disney or the irony of reusing it for a Disney production.[30] Beyoncé was trying to do something more by centering the song amidst other African musicians in a film celebrating the continent.

*Making the Gift* also becomes a kind of travelogue for her family's African adventures, as she describes her motivations and inspirations for each of the songs. While she works with artists from many different countries and we see her collaborating on the music in South Africa, she mostly only references 'Africa'. The story she tells of bringing her family home to Africa is a familiar one for Black Americans, who like her might experience an "ancestral connection to a land they come from and to people who share the same blood" (in her words). Yet the story veers consistently to an idea of Africa defined by a universalized unique spirit, best understood through its rhythms and vibrations. The accompanying images could be from any edgy tourist Instagram page, turned into mythic landscapes with gorgeous veldt and acacia trees, dirt roads leading on forever, city streets that are not quite western or fully urban, and oh, the children running, grinning and dancing.

Beyoncé stalks tattooed like an imaginary African Queen amidst happy and joyful, yet poor, people. Her narration evokes a blood connection to the land (Johannesburg's airport?) that brings her peace, but it always returns to the drums and the rhythms. She describes how she sought African artists and collaborators because she did not want to lose the "authenticity of Africa that starts with the drumbeat and the groove".

**Black is King**

The visual album – *Black is King* – roughly retells the story of *The Lion King* through a series of music videos songs rearranged from *The Gift*.[31] Directed by Emmanuel Adjei, Blitz Bazawule and Ibra Ake for the streaming channel Disney+, *Black is King* was written by Beyoncé, English poet Yrsa Daley-Ward, Guyanese-American music journalist Clover Hope and American writer Andrew Morrow, who also collaborated on Beyoncé's *Lemonade*. Stars from the United States, as well as from Nigeria, Cameroon, Ghana and South Africa, produced and/or wrote the music.[32] It also includes poetry by Somali-British poet Warsan Shire.[33] Blue Ivy Carter joins her mother, as well as fashion icon Naomi Campbell, Nigerian actress Lupita Nyong'o and Beyoncé's fellow Destiny's Child, Kelly Rowland on 'Brown Skin Girl'. The film is full of these familial and celebrity cameos.

Most of the film tells the basic story of *The Lion King* through a stylized narrative of a young African prince. He is swept up into a sinister world that takes him from the rural 'good Africa' to the dingy cityscapes of a distressed postcolonial Africa under the influence of powerful 'urban' Africans and finally grows up to realize his place in the royal stratosphere. The first song, 'Bigger', opens with a Moses-like rescue of a baby as Beyoncé narrates "Your roots and your story will be reborn". The film as a whole is clearly meant to evoke a Pan-Africa spirit as Claire Shaffer describe in her review for *Rolling Stone* magazine. This is marked by the use of an American flag colored black, red and green and a cornucopia of styles recognizable as 'traditional African', such as Himba ochre body and hair paint or 'contemporary African' like Nigerian afro-fusion choreography.[34] The visual album ends with a return to *The Gift* soundtrack, including the words of American and African collaborators and grounded in the struggles and joys of American Blackness.

African locations include the National Arts Theatre in Lagos, South Africa's Shakaland Zulu Village in KwaZulu-Natal (a theme park and hotel built around a television set) and the Ndebele church in Mapoch. Other sites included Ponte City apartments in Johannesburg and musician Shatta Wale's hometown of Nima, Ghana. Costume designer Zerina Akers drew on historical sources from Africa in order, she says, to create a global set of connections.[35] These include aesthetic inspirations already important to Black Americans like the cowry shells used as currency in the slave trade; Kanaga masks inspired by Dogon people's engagement with astronomy and the cosmos; and colors based on the Orishan idea of the Seven African Powers. Akers also drew from the style of women across the continent, such as Ndebele neck rings and Dahomey Amazons from what is now Benin and Nigerian matriarchal women's Jérôme blue Nigerian lace. Despite these inspirations and collaborations, the film's imagery steers very close to the classic tropes of western imaginings of Africa. Not only is the young prince eventually dressed as a Zulu king with leopard and cow skin familiar to fans of Shaka Zulu, Beyoncé wears a Burberry cow print top and skirt.

The key framing idea for the film comes from a poem by student Joshua Abah, *Uncle Sam*, that centers Black America's desire to know itself through a search for its mother tongue. What matters is Blackness in America where Black can be king, a powerful and beautiful sentiment for Americans.

## African Artists/African Worlds

In a wonderful reading of Beyoncé's stylistic evocation of Nigerian Goddesses along with Tanisha Ford's *Liberated Threads*, then Duke undergraduate student, Chinyere Amanze explored how African American struggles against a white aesthetic has had a long history of exploring style from Africa.[36] In her Grammy performance, for example, Beyoncé was quite literally embodying the sacred to express a message about the holiness of women and motherhood. The singer's choice to embody deities specifically from the African continent speaks to a more general association between the black sacred body and the continent.[37] But, as Amanze argues, these become removed from the specific sites of political and social struggles in different African countries in the interest of supporting a universalizing Black aesthetic, one that requires Africa to be seen only in terms of its pre/noncolonial history and existence.[38] To recognize the work of white supremacy on the continent risks stripping it of its power to liberate Americans. "This homogenizing and obscuring of the continent leave no room for the modern-day Nigeria or modern-day Mali where Fulani peoples may wear traditional nose adornments, but may also wear a t-shirt and blue jeans."[39]

Whether borrowing or inspiring, *Black is King* offers a beautiful, expansive, introduction to African iconography in hair, design, landscapes, architecture, make up and, indeed, rhythms and choreography. Such images are powerful in a pop cultural landscape that has largely marginalized the rich history of African style and art. But it doesn't just resonate with colonial imagery, it also borrows from contemporary African artists and has been accused of specifically stealing from South African based Congolese artist Petit Noir's 'Bigger Spirit' video for his album, *La Maison Noir*. On online forums people writing from the continent are generally clear that there is unacknowledged theft of styling, choreography and set up.[40] In many ways, the similarities do seem to go beyond an extraction of generic 'African' motifs and motions. The framing shot for shot is just too similar across the entirety of the two videos. These accusations have not been taken to court and might not be resolved on any legalistic level or be confirmed as plagiarism given the ways artists always borrow or find inspiration in all things. After all, little is in fact original. Beyoncé's supporters defend such borrowing using a language of celebration and homage to artists like Petit Noir or African aesthetics in general, making claims that creativity has no borders. It is chilling to note the sentiments that African artists should be grateful for the exposure Beyoncé is giving them, for example @karenclewski21 writes:

> This video and album as a whole pays homage to Africa and all its glory ... you are all part of that glory. ... She is bringing world wide recognition to your Art, the culture and traditions. ... She loves your art and wants to represent.

This, it seems, is her gift.

This tension is not incidental to thinking about the work of an album like *Black is King*. That Black Americans defend the film's borrowed inspirations based on the gift of exposure she is giving artists as opposed to making them equal collaborators on every level is made possible by the very geopolitical power that the United States and its citizen hold over Africans. This idea that an American can save an African musician's work from exploitation by Americans in a film primarily about American Blackness simply frames the ways even these forms of representation of Africa sustain a Savior Industrial Complex. It reflects a taken for granted sense of owning the privilege to speak on behalf of, and for, all Black people. Yes, it celebrates Blackness by rooting it in a deep African history and a pan-African collage of all things beautiful in music, movement and design, much as *Black Panther*'s costume design does. But the fine line between inspiration and copying and the implication that what is obviously African is somehow ancestral in a global economy where all is monetized to unequal benefits ensures that what is celebrated hides the exploitation of the continent.

## Imaging African Futures/Pasts

*Black is King* is celebrated for its Afrofuturism, in the sense that, like the work of science fiction writer Octavia Butler, it imagines a world where Black power is articulated through memories of the past and especially African heritages.[41] The film's celebration of Black and Brown beauty and power is apparent, and it grounds that power in an imagined African past. This past, like in *Black Panther*, is of a world preceding or outside of colonization or at least a world decorated in the iconography of an imagined pre-modern Africa. First, of course as the costumes make clear, this is a singular space where beauty and style are born out of multiple geographic and chronological sites. In some cases, they are inspired by stunning contemporary design by African artists, choreographers and filmmakers. In other scenes animal skins, cowry shells, desert landscapes, grass covered bodies, cow horns, chalky white painted skins, and green tribal-style markings also evoke the makeup used in Alicia Keys' Keep a Child Alive 'I am African' campaign. Such imagery put us firmly into a past Africa with no chronological or geographic distinctions.

It is through the use of ethnographic film styling and screening that the film disrupts its potential to reframe a Blackness as articulated with a contemporary and empowered Africa. Much of the creativity and beauty used in set and costume design is framed as quite literally primitive, given an ethnographic film blocking and color treatment. This is especially marked right at the beginning when Beyoncé lovingly carries a child along a beach in the first video for 'Bigger'. When the scene shifts to show Black women (dressed as generic traditional/rural Africans) leaning maternally over children the film stutters, decreases in frame size, and gains a sepia brown/ green color. This technical visual shift frames the women as objects in a 19th century-like ethnographic film. This gesture happens at multiple moments in *Black is King*, reminding the viewer of the long history of Westerners pointing cameras at exotic Africans producing a lexicon of film about Africa grounded in images of semi-naked, dancing, drumming or hunting Black people. This visual format evokes the colonial era films or the earlier ethnographic films by anthropologists trying to represent the exotic otherness of people in Africa and elsewhere through the lens of empire. It also creates a sense of watching films made to evoke horror or sympathy in equal amount to raise funds for missionary and other colonial expansion. This visual technique is shocking in its reminder of colonial era violence.[42]

In celebrating Africa by leap frogging centuries of colonial encounters and violence, as well as decades of postcolonial successes and failures, *Black is King* like *Black Panther* insists that African beauty and autonomy lie entirely in its past. Even the contemporary palatial site of '4Eva' reads more *Out of Africa*[43] luxury safari than a specific place in time. When we are clearly in an urban landscape, the imagery ensures that we only see a blasted cityscape. By filming in Ponte Towers, for example, the film takes a post-apartheid Johannesburg urban landmark already primed to represent decay and dissolution. It is a recognizable from the films of South African director Neill Blomkamp, for example, like *District 9* and especially *Chappie* that have made the building shorthand for a certain kind of Africa, not safari Africa but urban jungle Africa.[44] *Black is King*, however, mostly offers the beautiful expansive landscape and colorful historical culture that the travelers I studied looked for when they were seeking an Africa to celebrate. Twenty years ago, the travelers from the US that I interviewed believed that African success and wellbeing were visible where Africa was at its most primitive.[45] So a 'cultural village' where a chief can welcome visitors to his village no matter how poverty stricken or patriarchal is a sign of South African success while a township, no matter how diverse and economically active, is a blatant failure, sentiments that are rife in *Black is King*.

Beyoncé's responses to working with African artists on the continent echo the African Studies and Documentary Studies students' (at Duke in 2020) responses to the prompt: "When I Say Africa, what does this mean to you?" Here are some examples from the class exercises:

> I think of the music that takes from African traditions and sounds.
>
> I think of drums and bongos and layered rhythms; the traditional shout circles that carry into today's music.
>
> Traditional African dance/music/attire. . . . There's huge variation in this between Africa's subcultures so it's really more of a flashback of what I've personally witnessed.

Similarly to the students, as well as many of the travelers to southern Africa I observed 20 years ago, Beyoncé explains in the *Making the Gift* documentary how she wanted to be sure to "capture the dance culture of Africa" as she discovers that "there is a freedom to the way you dance" in Africa. She extolls the artistry of the "women of Northern Kenya" who made her daughter's "costumes" for an event. While the film occasionally tells us that an artist is in Nigeria or South Africa, Kenya is the only particular place Beyoncé names.

This language shows how much Beyoncé's engagement with the continent is flattened out in the all too familiar way that imperialists have written about, photographed and filmed in the past. By exploiting the music of many well-established artists from across the continent, but never in her mind losing the authenticity of Africa, what with its drumbeat and groove, Beyoncé feels like she has captured for the very first time for global audiences the sounds of Africa. Her hubris is redolent in her claim that she alone, disregarding a long history of extraction and collaborations by Westerners with African artists, has discovered the drums, chants and new sounds of Africa and by mixing them with producers from America has created her own genres.[46]

Despite her many collaborations with African musicians and artists in these projects, *Black is King*'s imagining of Africa remains grounded in a deeply American narrative about Blackness. Africa is where *Beyoncé belongs*. Her belonging is a gift, but a gift to who exactly? That she evokes the language of generosity so familiar in humanitarian engagements with Africa might be entirely an accident, but it still manages to turn the creative labor of African artists that could be an artistic collaboration, highly paid I am sure, into a gesture of kindness. In this context, when Africans and Americans work together, they are not so much building a product together but giving an American person the opportunity to help African musicians. *Black is King* is a spectacular production that works to incorporate black women but exclude African women, as US Malawian scholar, Priscilla Takondwa Semphere writes:

> Yet, *Black is King* sits uncomfortably. Like much of Bey's highly curated persona, it is evident to this African woman, that I am likely not included in her imagined audience. Africa and its people are peripheral props in her version of Blackness.[47]

This is the essence of a humanitarian construct that itself benefits from funding and organizational power, even as it hides the need for structural change to empower Africans. In the present unequal postcolonial world, the insistence that American Blackness is a globally unifying force, reveals the extent to which American Blackness constitutes an element of the Savior Industrial Complex. Simply substituting black for white devoid of a history of power and control, it reaffirms the ways that Americanness and Whiteness are articulated.

## Un/Real Africa

I explored how humanitarian parody and critique expose American parochialism in Chapter 2. Here I have used sites of American pop culture celebrating Blackness to think through what happens to Africa when it is imagined as a way to tell American stories. I focus on a global Blackness grounded in American imaginings of Africa rather than the multiple other complex sites interweaving diasporas, ocean crossings and enslavements.[48] Or as Semphere writes in her essay on *Black is King* for the online magazine *Africa is a Country*:

> In recent years, themes centering the African heritage of Black people globally have gained prominence in popular media. Yet Western media remains hegemonic and Western sensibilities continue to be privileged. This means that even films and TV shows that purport to center Black people who are also Africans (Black Africans) are not for us. As Black American identity in particular has "gone global," with Beyoncé as its chief ambassador, Black Africans have had to learn to make do with morsels of representation. No matter how carefully curated, and no matter how breathtakingly delivered, images of Africa continue to be deeply problematic, hewing to old, frustrating tropes.[49]

In their essay on 'Beyoncé and the Heart of Darkness' for *Africa is a Country*, Boluwatife Akinro and Joshua Segus-Lean also ask:

> Would a Zamunda without its prosperity or a Wakanda without the technological advancements of vibranium be of much interest to African-American audiences? It would seem that none of the Africas the rest of the world imagines are any of the ones Africans live and think and work and love and die in.[50]

They echo here my concern that the celebration of an imagined Africa in *Black Panther* and *Black is King* risks fostering the erasure of African belonging so patent in tourists' search for the perfect shot of a lion and in the creation of Wakanda as an idealized landscape without colonized Africans.

Semphere acknowledges that in the context of US racism and anti-black violence, such questions of representation and conversations about who performs whom and who represents Black American experience matter. But she takes issue with how this conversation can create rifts among global Black communities rather than forge connections grounded in shared histories of oppression. As she argues:

> What comes at issue then is not this definition of self – it is the erasure that inevitably happens when the span of our understanding of blackness does not encapsulate or demonstrate an awareness of the

experience of black non-Americans in and outside of America. It therefore becomes that in order to be seen, heard, celebrated or even advocated for, other forms of living and existing as black must bend to some of these common understandings, that are often tinged with a strange, ironic cousin of nationalism one might call black exclusivity.[51]

## Saving America

I have frequently argued that travel to Africa, popular representations of the continent and the drive to save Africans depend on, maintain and reproduce a narrative that excises Africans from the landscape and empties it out for the benefit of Americans' sense of belonging. Chapter 1 summarized the ways travel made it possible for Americans to find their best selves in Africa through this gesture of emptying its landscapes of Africans or Africanness. Anybody or anything that did not mesh with their imagined Africa, the one that needed them or needed America, was simply declared not the 'real Africa' by travelers. When Bono declared that Africa is burning and only 'we' can save it or Disney's Africa resides in their Animal Kingdom safari and poacher hunter adventure, Americans can engage with an Africa empty of Africans with agency.[52] This trope remains at the heart of Ryan Coogler's *Black Panther* – a film that makes clear we understand that Wakanda is not 'that Africa'.[53]

Much of the film's dramatic arc plays out through the argument between T'Challa and his cousins. Both Killmonger and W'Kabi are frustrated at how isolated Wakanda is and how little it does for the rest of the world. While T'Challa is persuaded to share their wealth, he (and the film) maintains that their power lies in their exceptional status on the continent. Ultimately, he returns to Killmonger's neighborhood in Oakland to establish Wakandan's humanitarian projects. The message is that there is no saving a colonized Africa; Africa is only good when its history is eradicated. But ultimately, this prefigures the entanglements between Barbie Savior, white saviors and the Black people they claim to be helping. In some ways, Priest was ahead of the game in creating a white savior who was intrinsically funny and, therefore, both sympathetic and unthreatening. This gesture weaves even more closely these narratives of powerful black characters with those of the white savior whose ability to laugh and mock themselves disguises their neocolonial actions.

In pushing back against the focus on US-centered diasporan concerns Nigerian American author Ndedi Okorofor defines her own writing about diasporic Blackness as 'Africanfuturism', which does not demand that Wakanda save Oakland but centers a more complex diaspora and the life in Africa itself.[54] While imagining connections across the diaspora is entirely necessary, I believe it matters who controls those imaginings, and why and what gives them power to do that. The aspirations of an Africa outside of colonialism and with the power to push back against contemporary forms of imperialism is from the perspective of the United States a purely marvelous thing and shows the power of pop culture in imagining different futures and even different pasts. Anthony Faramelli closely disarticulates the ways *Black Panther* sets two American struggles for Black power against each other – resistance or revolution. He suggests that "T'Challa did die when Killmonger threw him from the waterfall during ritual combat. T'Challa the conservative isolationist died so that T'Challa the progressive liberal could be born".[55] For him, too, the result is a humanitarian state, though one rescued by T'Challa's lover, Nakia, a strong Black woman who pushes for a 'better' more revolutionary way to do aid.

## *Unbearable Whiteness*

My focus, perforce of course, must be Whiteness and how saving Africa articulates Whiteness to all Americans. The foundational work on Whiteness in the American academy called out the ways Whiteness is rendered invisible due to its power and privilege.[56] Peggy McIntosh described white privilege as "an invisible weightless knapsack of provisions, maps, guides, codebooks, passports, visas, compasses and blank checks".[57] I argued in my book on travelers that this is a kind of privilege that is accessed by all Americans, who can move through or imagine the world with their own invisible backpacks of privilege with its very real passports, visas and check cards so coveted by many elsewhere in the world. These backpacks make visible how Americanness is a location of political domination on a global, rather than local, scale. It is that act of Whiteness that I suggest is often overlooked in the evocation of the White Savior (Industrial) Complex and especially when white supremacy is evoked.

I suggest that when *Black Panther* and *Black is King* become sites of erasure, this reveals the ways that Americanness is articulated with Whiteness and that Whiteness' relationship with Africa is one of simultaneous extracting and helping. Witness Beyoncé's collaborations with African artists as her 'gift' or of Black Panther's new humanitarian project in Oakland. These cloaked messages reflect, I argue, the same kind of white supremacy that Jemima Pierre's ethnography exposes in Ghana.[58] Using Ghana as a site and proximate for Africa and Pan-Africanism, Pierre argues that local configurations of race are structured through global hierarchical relationships. She suggests that Whiteness is a constructed entity whose privileges can be accessed mainly by those born into the area (those with white skin) but also by non-whites who strive to achieve proximity through performance.

Whiteness is not only a matter of individual genealogies but is grounded in place and in politics. Pierre highlights a link between commodities, consumptions and the performance of Whiteness to access some of the fruits of white privilege.[59] As its history in the United States shows, Whiteness is made, at least for some, because Americanness is Whiteness.[60]

I suggest that Americanness and Whiteness are so inextricably linked that the ways Black Americans exploit ideas of Africa to overcome their own marginalization reproduce the same tired tropes that position Africans as powerless and silent. In an essay on Rachel Dolezal's discomfiting claims of a transracial identity to justify her performance of Blackness and especially her commitment to saving Black lives, Aldous Reed writes: "that the Dolezal issue has captured such attention only because it rankles the sensibilities of those who essentialize race and that no one is making her talk about it but herself".[61] It is these kinds of performances that expose how imagining a particular kind of Africa in order to emancipate Blackness in America can become intertwined and dependent on Whiteness. Beyoncé is performing white power, although it is embodied by Blackness. While these performances reflect how starved Black Americans are for positive representations, American pop culture simultaneously denies the foundations of Black poverty while exploiting fantasy images of Blackness that deny the sin of colonization.

## Belonging in America

The White Savior Industrial Complex is able to reinvent itself as satire or parody, happily, as I suggest in the previous chapters, co-existing with its own critique and creating spaces for a seemingly self-aware politics of doing good. Rather than make explicit the ways that white privilege is not the individual luckiness of being white but the ways that political, social and economic structures are built around and for white people, the overuse of terms like white supremacy have worked to make it seem as if using it puts you outside of it. It is this act of Whiteness that does not depend on white people alone.[62] The parodies, of course, also show how easy it is to mock Whiteness with all of its self-absorbed self-loathing that does little to dismantle the system that creates so much privilege in the first place. You can look silly and still be in power. This is in part because a critique dependent on satirical hypernormalization helps to distance participants from the problem. So white folk continue to produce ideas about Africa that position them as the best thing for Africans while never addressing the geopolitical structures that ensure their own privilege. While the White Savior Industrial Complex might rest on white privilege, it can be enacted by Black Americans like Oprah, as Teju Cole makes clear in his tweets on the

White Savior Industrial Complex: "4 – This world exists simply to satisfy the needs – including, importantly, the sentimental needs – of white people and Oprah".[63] This is not just because a global icon like Oprah transcends all categories, but is, in part, made possible by her Americanness.

What this means for people of color in the United States is a perpetual second-class citizenship that brings marginalization, violence and struggle. Yet what can be elided in the struggles for Black lives in the US is that when looking from outside, in decentering the American experience, it is also possible to see how Black Americans enact and experience some of the privileges and the power of global Whiteness. Though deeply complex and varied, I am only thinking through here how these privileges play out in the ways that Americans imagine Africa. I suggest that pop cultural phenomena, like *Black Panther* and *Black is King*, assume that American struggles over Blackness and belonging are universal and normalized struggles that appear to require little translation as they cross borders.

*Black Panther*, after all, creates a place in Africa for Westerners black and white to journey to where colonialism does not exist. Wakanda is most marked by its outsiderness: outside of colonialism, outside of contemporary imperialism, outside of all forms of western extraction, its entire purpose in fact is to protect its metal and its technologies from these forces. At T'Challa's challenge for the leadership early in the film, Wakandans gather in all their glory. The men are powerful and the women gorgeous, and we know we are in Africa. This moment, stunning as it is, does some of the ugliest work in the movie in its representation of Africans. We already know that Wakanda sees itself as apart from the rest of Africa, which is simply dismissed as hopeless, war mongering, poverty ridden and with basically no agency. Yet Wakanda's various 'tribes' stand in for multiple people who have achieved social and political wealth historically but also in the present, represented by their design sensibilities and their production of artwork and materials. These are recognizable but only in a generic this-is-Africa fashion. Africa as a whole is essentially lost while inhabiting a smorgasbord of pan-African wonders, uncredited to the specific regions or eras from which they were appropriated.

When *Black is King* uses the style and framing of colonial early 20th century film, including the cutting of the screen, a complete change in color and tone, the absence of chains and violence is disturbing. While it might mean something awfully subtle, it speaks to a tone deafness about how to tell stories about Africa that is made possible by Americanness. Too much of *Black is King* seems to be saying 'look at the beautiful deep history of Africans, their style, strength, rhythms'. But that is surely offensive when the colonial history of violence is erased, and the specific stories of the people are denied in the interest of a spiritual tale of kingship or queenship.

Ndlovu-Gatsheni and Pinki Ndlovu argue that coloniality is an active global power that structures and sustains the dominance of the Global North over the Global South, producing in many African countries a kind of neo-colonialism perpetrated by a black bourgeoisie.[64] In similar ways to how these postcolonial leaders in Africa succumbed to the systemic power of global white supremacy, currently African leaders ground themselves in the very systems used to marginalize, dehumanize and colonize black people all over the world, creating elites that seem to prove a post racial world. The United States is perhaps the colony that is least decolonized, not least because it seldom looks hard at itself as a settler colony.[65]

While both *Black Panther* and Beyoncé's work can be read and experienced as an aspirational dream for Africans, it also reiterates the ways western desires are for a future without African's own burdens of their dark and violent histories. As Schmidt argues in an essay exploring anti-colonialism and feminism in *Black Panther*: "T'Challa has to fight Killmonger because in confronting him he is combating a particular, partly American-formed vision of Black power that says victory can only be achieved via a Black empire of world domination and subjugation that outdoes all previous colonial empires".[66] Colonialism absolutely devastated Africa; imperialism and capitalism continues to do so, but if we really want to imagine an emancipated way of being African it has to build on and incorporate this history, not deny it. It has to be through colonialism, not instead of it. By siting power in uncolonized Black spaces only, Wakanda and *Black is King* do not give Africans that opportunity. They make clear as powerfully as Bono does that Africans cannot save themselves. These fantasies have enormous value for what it means to be Black in America. But just like the fantasy of the White Savior Industrial Complex, it depends on eradicating particular and geographically diverse lives in Africa. Africans, after all, live in a world that was most certainly colonized and continues to be a site of resource extraction in all of its ugliest forms. Wakanda and *Black is King* suggest that living through that has made Africans irrelevant, helpless and hopeless.

These configurations become visible in the ways that Africa is mobilized in Black American pop culture. The deeply embedded structures of white privilege in postcolonial Africa that ensure continuing and profoundly influential racist structures to define life for Africans after the end of formal colonial structures means that white bodies are no longer necessary for white supremacy to thrive. In much the same way, white bodies are no longer necessary for the White Savior Industrial Complex to thrive. Similarly, to elite Africans, Black Americans have been profoundly exploited and violated but also implicated in the project of American empire and have gained resources and privileges founded in white supremacy while not always acknowledging the cost to Black and Brown people elsewhere in the world.

One of the many violences of American Whiteness, I suggest, is the ways it incorporates Black Americans, whether they like it or not, supporting the ways that they imagine Africa from empire's center. Looking from the south reveals the extent to which America is behind in decolonizing Black lives or (re)membering Black humanity.[67]

## Notes

1. Priest, Christopher and Joe Quesada. 2015. *Black Panther by Christopher Priest*. The Complete Collection Vol. 1. Issues 1–17. New York: Marvel Entertainment.
2. This complicated history of Black Americans seeking self in Africa is partially found in these diverse texts: Angelou, Maya. 1991. *All God's Children Need Traveling Shoes*. Vintage. Reprint edition, Blyden, Nemata Amelia Ibitayo. 2019. *African Americans and Africa: A New History*. New Haven: Yale University Press, Ebron, Paulla A. 1999. 'Tourists as Pilgrims: Commercial Fashioning of Transatlantic Politics.' *American Ethnologist*, 26: 910–932, Holsey, Bayo. 2008. *Routes of Remembrance: Refashioning the Slave Trade in Ghana*. Chicago: University of Chicago Press. Chapter 6. 'Slavery and the Making of Black Atlantic History' and Richburg, Keith B. 1997. *Out of America: A Black Man Confronts Africa*. New York: Basic Books.
3. See for example Contreras, Russel. 2021. 'How Black Lives Matter Helped Native Americans and Latinos.' *Politics & Policy*, March 13, 2021 and Trent, Sydney. 2020. 'Young Asians and Latinos Push Their Parents to Acknowledge Racism Amid Protests.' *The Washington Post*, June 22, 2020.
4. See for example: Aldama, Frederick Luis and Christopher González. 2019. *Reel Latinxs: Representation in U.S. Film and TV*. Tucson: University of Arizona Press, Erigha, Maryann. 2019. *The Hollywood Jim Crow: The Racial Politics of the Movie Industry*. New York: NYU Press, Lopez, Lori Kido. 2016. *Asian American Media Activism: Fighting for Cultural Citizenship*. New York: NYU Press and Mahdi, Waleed F. 2020. *Arab Americans in Film: From Hollywood and Egyptian Stereotypes to Self-Representation*. Syracuse University Press.
5. See some summary histories here: Adi, Hakim. 2018. *Pan-Africanism: A History*. Bloomsbury Academic, Bloom, Joshua and Waldo E. Martin Jr. 2016. *Black against Empire: The History and Politics of the Black Panther Party*. Berkeley: University of California Press, Martin, Tony. 2020. *Race First: The Ideological and Organizational Struggles of Marcus Garvey and the Universal Negro Improvement Association*. Baltimore, MD: Black Classic Press.
6. Some examples from around the world: Alade, Olujimi. 2020. 'Black Lives Matter – from Nigeria to the U.S.' *Mundo Obrero. Workers World*, November 11, 2020. www.workers.org/2020/11/52396/; Brown, Ashley Brown. 2020. 'Vidas Negras Importam: The Black Lives Matter Movement in Brazil.' *Panoramas*. www.panoramas.pitt.edu/news-and-politics/vidas-negras-importam-black-lives-matter-movement-brazil. Accessed October 22, 2021; Donkor, Audrey. 2020. 'Black Lives Must Matter in Africa Too.' *Mail & Guardian*, July 19, 2020. https://mg.co.za/africa/2020-07-19-black-lives-must-matter-in-africa-too/; Nagumo, Jada and Nana Shibata. 2020. '#BlackLivesMatter Shines Light on Racism in Japan and Across Asia.' *Nikkei Asia*, August 11, 2020 04:01 JST. https://asia.nikkei.com/Spotlight/Asia-Insight/BlackLivesMatter-shines-light-on-racism-in-Japan-and-across-Asia. Accessed October 22, 2021.

7. Keys, Rob. 2013. 'Is Marvel Studios Actively Searching to Cast "Black Panther"? Chadwick Boseman Tops the Rumored Shortlist.' *ScreenRant*, May 1, 2013, Smith, Jamil. 2018. 'The Revolutionary Power of *Black Panther*: Marvel's New Movie Marks a Major Milestone.' *TIME*, February 19, 2018. https://time.com/black-panther/.
8. Celebrating casting of Black actors in Black roles via the trending #BlackPantherSoLIT hashtag; Verhoeven, Beatrice. 2016. 'Michael B. Jordan's 'Black Panther' Casting Sparks #BlackPantherSoLIT Hashtag on Twitter.' *The Wrap*, May 14, 2016 @ 9:38 AM. www.thewrap.com/michael-b-jordans-black-panther-casting-sparks-blackpanthersolit-hashtag-on-twitter/.
9. Priest and Quesada, 2015. Emphasis in original.
10. Reisman, Abraham. 2018. 'Christopher Priest Made Black Panther Cool then Disappeared.' *Vulture*, January 22, 2018. www.vulture.com/2018/01/christopher-priest-made-black-panther-cool-then-disappeared.html.
11. See for example the Reddit Imaginary Maps; r/imaginarymaps and Hill, James and Nick Jones. 2021. *Marvel Universe Map by Map*. London: DK.
12. A conversation that also animates commentary on the film: Beauchamp, Zack. 2018. 'What Black Panther Can Teach us about International Relations.' *VOX*, February 27, 2018. www.vox.com/culture/2018/2/27/17029730/black-panther-marvel-killmonger-ir, Eisenberg, Eric. 2018. 'How Black Panther's Cast Feels About the Controversial Wakanda Border Debate.' *Cinema Blend*, February 7, 2018. www.cinemablend.com/news/2307371/how-black-panthers-cast-feels-about-the-controversial-wakanda-border-debate.
13. Priest and Quesada, 2015. Emphasis in original.
14. Jesudason, David. 2021. 'Is Hollywood Ready to Stop Stereotyping Africa?' *BBC*, March 4, 2021. www.bbc.com/culture/article/20210304-is-hollywood-ready-to-stop-stereotyping-africa.
15. Coates, Ta-Nehesi and Brian Stelfreeze. 2016–2018. *Black Panther: A Nation Under Our Feet*. New York: Marvel. More recently Nigerian American writer Ndedi Okorofor has helmed women centered graphic novels centered on Wakanda such as *Shuri* and *Wakanda Forever* published by Marvel: www.marvel.com/comics/creators/13208/nnedi_okorafor.
16. Priest and Quesada. 2015. Ibid.
17. Tucker, Boima. 'Black America's Africa.' *Africa is a Country*, February 23, 2018. https://africasacountry.com/2018/02/african-americas-wakanda.
18. Quoted in Jesudason, 2021. Ibid.
19. Cobb, Jelani. 2018. '"Black Panther" and the Invention of "Africa".' *The New Yorker*, February 18, 2018. www.newyorker.com/news/daily-comment/black-panther-and-the-invention-of-africa.
20. Mutunga, Felix. 2020. 'Rethinking Africa-US Relations through the Entertainment Industry.' *Africa Portal*, October 15, 2020. www.africaportal.org/features/rethinking-africa-us-relations-through-entertainment-industry/.
21. Ayisi, Erica. 2018. 'Make Wakanda Real by Embracing Your African Roots.' *The ROOT*, March 5, 2018 10:00AM. www.theroot.com/make-wakanda-real-by-embracing-your-african-roots-1823498886.
22. Nyabola, Nanjala. 2018. 'Wakanda is Not African, and that's OK.' *AlJazeera*, March 13, 2018. www.aljazeera.com/opinions/2018/3/13/wakanda-is-not-african-and-thats-ok.
23. Thanks to one of my amazing International Comparative Studies student, Chinyere Amanze, for raising these questions.

24. See here for a discussion of the diaspora symbolism in the album: What Beyoncé teaches us about the African diaspora in 'Lemonade.' *PBS Canvas*, April 29, 2016 6:07 PM EDT. www.pbs.org/newshour/arts/what-beyonce-teaches-us-about-the-african-diaspora-in-lemonade.
25. See: Damola, Durosomo. 2017. 'Beyoncé Channeled the Yoruba Deities Oshun and Yemoja for Her Pregnancy Shoot.' *OKAYAFRICA*, February 03, 2017 08:35PM EST. www.okayafrica.com/beyonce-channeled-yoruba-goddess-oshun-maternity-photoshoot/.
26. Beyoncé, Blitz the Ambassador, Kwasi Fordjour, Emmanuel Adjei, Jenn Nkiru, Ibra Ake, Jake Nava. 2020. *Black is King*. Parkwood Entertainment; Walt Disney Pictures.
27. #BEYONCÉ #TheGift #TheLionKing Making the Gift. Documentary. Beyoncé Music. September 17, 2019. www.youtube.com/watch?v=daNaICPI_7M. Accessed July 19, 2020.
28. Favreau, Jon. 2019. *The Lion King*. Walt Disney Pictures and Fairview Entertainment.
29. Akosuba, Tokoni. 2020. 'Why Beyoncé Made "Black Is King" – Tina Knowles.' *Eelive*, August 6, 2020. www.eelive.ng/why-beyonce-made-black-is-king-tina-knowles/.
30. Ratiba, Matome M. 2012. '"The Sleeping Lion Needed Protection" – Lessons from the Mbube (Lion King) Debacle.' *Journal of International Commercial Law and Technology*, 7(1): 1–10.
31. Track List for *Black is King*:
    1. Bigger (ft. RAYE)
    2. Find Your Way Back
    3. Don't Jealous Me (by Tekno, Yemi Alade and Mr. Eazi)
    4. Ja Ara E (by Burna Boy)
    5. Nile (with Kendrick Lamar)
    6. Mood 4 Eva (ft. Childish Gambino, Jay-Z and Oumou Sangare)
    7. Brown Skin Girl (with SAINT JHN and Wizkid) (ft. Blue Ivy Carter)
    8. Keys to the Kingdom (by Tiwa Savage and Mr. Eazi)
    9. Already (with Shatta Wale and Major Lazer)
    10. Otherside
    11. My Power (ft. Busiswa, Moonchild Sanelly, Nija, Tierra Whack and Yemi Alade)
    12. Scar (by 070 Shake and Jessie Reyez)
    13. Spirit
    14. Black Parade (extended)
    15. Find Your Way Back (MeLo-X remix) (ft. MeLo-X)
    16. Black Parade
32. Vargas, Chanel. 2020. 'From Blue Ivy to Wizkid, See all the Artists Featured on Beyonce's Black is King Visual Album.' *Pop Sugar*. www.popsugar.com/entertainment/beyonce-black-is-king-featured-artists-47659784.
33. Adjei, Emmanuel, Ibra Ake and Bliz Bazawule. 2020. *Black is King*. Walt Disney Pictures, Parkwood Entertainment, Hamlet.
34. Shaffer, Claire. 2020. '5 Takeaways From Beyonce's Elaborate New Visual Album "Black Is King".' *Rolling Stone*, July 31, 2020 8:31AM ET. www.rollingstone.com/music/music-features/beyonce-black-is-king-disney-1036650/.
35. Gardner, Chris. 2020. 'Beyonce's "Black Is King" Costume Designer Unpacks Cultural References, Favorite Style Moments.' *The Hollywood Reporter*,

August 5, 2020, 12:51 PM. www.hollywoodreporter.com/news/music-news/beyonce-black-is-king-costume-designer-interview-1305461/.
36. Ford, Tanisha C. 2015. *Liberated Threads: Black Women, Style, and the Global Politics of Soul*. Chapel Hill: University of North Carolina Press.
37. Reviewed in Tucker Edmonds, Joseph L. 2018. 'The Canonical Black Body: Alternative African American Religions and the Disruptive Politics of Sacrality.' *Religions*, 9(1): 17. http://doi.org/10.3390/rel9010017.
38. Ellen McLarney struggles with these tensions in her analysis of Beyonce's Lemonade that strikes at the heart of American anti-Blackness and misogyny while struggling to acknowledge the marginalization of even her own collaborators: McLarney, Ellen. 2019. 'Beyoncé's Soft Power: Poetics and Politics of an Afro-Diasporic Aesthetics.' *Camera Obscura 101*, 34(2): 1–39.
39. Some of my amazing International Comparative Studies seniors worked through these ideas in their research papers, and I am especially indebted to Chinyere Amanze and Helen Yu for their thoughtful critiques.
40. Chronicle Speaks does a great job outlining the debate here: Beyonce STOLE Video Idea From South African Artist For Spirit + Bigger Video? – *YouTube*, July 22, 2019.
41. See for example: Gipson, Grace. 2019. 'Creating and Imagining Black Futures through Afrofuturism.' In *#Identity: Hashtagging Race, Gender, Sexuality, and Nation*, ed. Abigail De Kosnik and Keith P. Feldman, 84–103. Ann Arbor: University of Michigan Press, Reed, Sabrina. 2020. 'Beyoncé's Black Is King Visual Album Embraces Afrofuturism.' *FanSided*. https://culturess.com/2020/07/21/beyonces-black-king-visual-album-embraces-afrofuturism/ and Woronzoff, Elisabeth. 2020. 'Beyoncé's "Black Is King" Builds Identity From Afrofuturism.' *Pop Matters*, August 3, 2020. www.popmatters.com/beyonce-black-is-king-review-2646867320.html.
42. Griffiths, Alison. 2002. *Wondrous Difference: Cinema, Anthropology & Turn-of-the-Century Visual Culture*. New York: Columbia University Press.
43. In many ways Meryl Streep's and Robert Redford's weepy visual based on Isak Dineson's memoir of living on a farm in Africa (Kenya) set the tone of post 1980s visual landscape for how to show your love affair with Africa: Pollack, Sydney. 1985. *Out of Africa*. Mirage Enterprises.
44. Blomkamp, Neill. 2015. *Chappie*. Columbia Pictures; Blomkamp, Neill. 2009, *District 9*. Tristar Pictures. See: Brown, Ryan Lenora. 2017. 'The South African Building That Came to Symbolize the Apocalypse.' *The Atlantic*, February 21, 2017. www.theatlantic.com/entertainment/archive/2017/02/the-south-african-building-that-came-to-symbolize-the-apocalypse/517056/.
45. Mathers, Kathryn. 2010. *Travel, Humanitarianism and Becoming American in Africa*. New York: Palgrave.
46. Thanks to Sean Jacobs' social media post that alerted me to this film and this claim.
47. Semphere, Takondwa. 2020. 'Beyond African Royalty.' *Africa is a Country*. https://africasacountry.com/2020/09/beyond-african-royalty.09.25.2020AIAC.
48. Hartman, Saidiya. 2008. *Lose Your Mother: A Journey Along the Atlantic Slave Route*. New York: Farrar, Straus and Giroux.
49. Semphere Takondwa. 2020. 'Beyond African Royalty.' *Africa is a Country*, September 25, 2020. https://africasacountry.com/2020/09/beyond-african-royalty.

50. Akinro, Boluwatife and Joshua Segun-Lean. 2019. 'Beyoncé and the Heart of Darkness.' *Africa is a Country*. https://africasacountry.com/2019/09/beyonces-heart-of-darkness. Accessed September 15, 2019.
51. Semphere, Priscilla Takondwa. 2017. 'Blacker Than You: Daniel Kaluuya, the Place of Race and the Race of Place.' *HuffPost*, March 16, 2017. www.huffpost.com/entry/blacker-than-you-daniel-kaluuya-the-place-of-race_b_58c99be8e4b0e0d348b33ff8.
52. Mathers, Kathryn. 2010. *Travel, Humanitarianism, and Becoming American in Africa*. New York: Palgrave.
53. Coogler, Ryan. 2018. *Black Panther*. Marvel Studios, Walt Disney Productions.
54. Okorafor, Nnedi. 2021. 'Africanfuturism Defined.' In *Africanfuturism: An Anthology*, ed. Wole Talabi. ebook. Brittle Paper. https://brittlepaper.com/2020/10/free-download-of-africanfuturism-an-anthology-stories-by-nnedi-okorafor-tl-huchu-dilman-dila-rafeeat-aliyu-tlotlo-tsamaase-mame-bougouma-dienemazi-nwonwu-and-derek-lubangakene/.
55. Faramelli, Anthony. 2019. 'Liberation on and Off Screen: Black Panther and Black Liberation Theory.' *Space, Place, and Identities Onscreen*, 43(2).
56. Frankenberg, Ruth. 1994. 'Whiteness and Americanness: Examining Constructions of Race, Culture and Nation in White Women's Life Narratives.' In *Race*, ed. S. Gregory and R. Sanjek. New Brunswick, NJ: Rutgers University Press, Kolchin, Peter. 2002. 'Whiteness Studies: The New History of Race in America.' *The Journal of American History*, 89(1): 154–173 and for a contemporary review on thinking about whiteness in the United States: Rankin, Claudia. 2020. *Just Us: An American Conversation*. Minneapolis: Graywolf Press.
57. McIntosh, Peggy. 1988. *White Privilege and Male Privilege: A Personal Account of Coming to See Correspondences Through Work in Women's Studies*. Wellesley, MA: Wellesley College Center for Research on Women.
58. Pierre, Jemima. 2012. *The Predicament of Blackness: Postcolonial Ghana and the Politics of Race*. Chicago: University of Chicago Press.
59. Thanks Helen Yu for thinking this through with me; Pierre, Jemima. 2012: 86. Ibid.
60. See for example Flores, William V. 2003. 'New Citizens, New Rights Undocumented Immigrants and Latino Cultural Citizenship.' *Latin American Perspectives*, 129, 30(3): 295–308, Lalami, Laila. 2020. *Conditional Citizens: On Belonging in America*. New York: Pantheon, McDermott, Monica. 2020. *Whiteness in America*. Cambridge, UK: Polity, Ong, Aiwha. 1996. 'Cultural Citizenship as Subject-Making: Immigrants Negotiate Racial and Cultural Boundaries in the United States.' *Current Anthropology*, 37(5): 737–762 and Roediger, David R. 2018. *Working Toward Whiteness: How America's Immigrants Became White: The Strange Journey from Ellis Island to the Suburbs*. New York: Basic Books.
61. Reed, Adolph J. 2015. 'From Jenner to Dolezal: One Trans Good, the Other Not So Much.' *Common Dreams*, June 15, 2015. www.commondreams.org/views/2015/06/15/jenner-dolezal-one-trans-good-other-not-so-much#
62. Steyn, Melissa and William Mpofu, eds. 2021. *Decolonising the Human: Reflections from Africa on Difference and Oppression*. Johannesburg: WITS University Press.
63. Cole, Teju. 2012. 'The White-savior Industrial Complex.' *The Atlantic*, March 21.

64. Ndlovu-Gatsheni, Sabelo J. and Patricia Pinky Ndlovu. 2021. 'The Invention of Blackness on a World Scale.' In *Decolonising the Human: Reflections from Africa on Difference and Oppression*, ed. Melissa Steyn and William Mpofu, 41. Johannesburg: WITS University Press.
65. See for example Dunbar-Ortiz, Roxanne. 2021. *Not "a Nation of Immigrants": Settler Colonialism, White Supremacy, and a History of Erasure and Exclusion.* Beacon, MA: Beacon Press.
66. Schmidt, Peter. 2019. ""Black Panther:" Some Thoughts on Anti-Colonialism, Feminism, Xhosa, and Black Pixels in the Film (With an Aside on Ava DuVernay's "A Wrinkle In Time").' *English Literature Faculty Works*. http://doi.org/10.24968/2476-2458.engl.346. https://works.swarthmore.edu/fac-english-lit/346.
67. Ndlovu-Gatsheni, Sabelo J. and Patricia Pinky Ndlovu. 2021: 26. Ibid.

# Conclusion

> What this scholarship does is demonstrate how the mobilization of America as object becomes clearest when it travels into the phantasmatic space of its putative opposite, Africa. More specifically, Americans become visible as subjects, as ways of being, and as ethical actors through a particular humanitarian comportment toward Africa. Just as the United States becomes visible through its (great white) hopefulness, Africa becomes invisible through its despair.[1]

In this review of *Travel, Humanitarianism, and Becoming American in Africa*,[2] my colleague, Sarah Cervenak, articulates both the beginning and the end of this new book, which reflects on my original research 20 years later. Amidst 2020's ongoing global pandemic and the United States' attempted reckoning with white supremacy, when both Africa and America inhabit a shared space of despair, I have to ask why, as Cervenak argues in the same review essay, Americanness still "becomes itself through the disavowal of difference [that is] at the core of its neocolonial relationship with 'Africa'".[3] I would add that this disavowal is also at the core of Americanness' relationship with itself.

I have explored seemingly divergent sites of American imaginings of Africa through popular culture that evolved in the wake of my earlier research and writing. I have actively attempted to redress how American media tells stories about Africa. I begin as I ended the previous book with travel, with its long history of creating an 'Africa' ripe for takeover, for extraction, for enslaving and for finding your savage and your truer self. Chapter 1 briefly compared the ways Americans travel then and now and how very little has changed. Travel and the images it produces continue to construct an Africa in need of saving and to raise questions about American imperialism and global white supremacy. I touched on the changes to the images created by major humanitarian brands like (RED) over the last 5 years. This shift was a response to critiques of representations of Africa that focused on suffering, hopelessness and need through the late 20th and even early 21st century. But, as I suggest, these calls for saving lives that depend on smiling black faces and hard-working black teachers and nurses in fact continue to depend on the unspoken assumptions of African suffering.[4] While the white expert from abroad is no longer front and center in these reframed fundraising videos, they remain in the background of these images as the caring consumer and donor. This careful erasure of the physical image of a white savior works to distance how African voices are erased from the industries of doing good and raising money or awareness.

In Chapter 2 I showed how voluntourism and consuming for good have become the primary site for Americans to find their best selves in Africa – a 21st century form of imperialist extraction. Despite the self-aware critiques, like Barbie Savior, that make the do-gooding voluntourism and compassionate consumption the butt of the jokes, travel and shopping continue to uphold a White Savior Industrial Complex. In unpacking the mobilization of parody to critique the White Savior Industrial Complex through social media sites like NORAID's Radiators for Norway campaigns and Barbie Savior, I show how Whiteness travels to reassert itself through critiques of feminized caring, hiding this powerful industrial complex in plain sight while continuing to silence Africans.

If Whiteness is central to both the extractive politics of saviorism as well as the critique of how it works, Chapter 3's exploration of the films *Black Panther* and *Black is King* suggests that this is a Whiteness so articulated with Americanness that it also influences Black popular culture. When white Americans laugh at their saviorism as a way to find themselves in Africa, and Black Americans use media and pop culture to travel to a reimagined Africa, they both sustain a White Savior Industrial Complex. As I show, the narratives and production of becoming a superhero of a lone, fictional African state or transforming to an African Goddess, unmoored from the specificity of economics and culture, requires an imaginary Africa emptied of colonial history and current economics. This articulation of positive Black American images so distanced from Black people outside the United States reflects the kind of "liberal multiculturalist common sense" that Dylan Rodríguez warned was beginning to show its colors with Barack Obama's election in 2008.[5] He articulates the violence then of simply changing the surface appearance while leaving the structures of oppression intact:

> While the phenotype of white supremacy changes – and change it must, if it is to remain viable under changed historical conditions – its

internal coherence as a socialized logic of violence and dominance is sustained and redeemed.

In the end, Americans produce a form of media representation that hypernormalizes, rather than undermines, the power of Whiteness.[6] This is the tension that brings me back to Whiteness as a site to explore the ways that parody and fantasy struggle to disrupt white supremacy.

I am, of course, aware of the problem of my own position, white and born, raised and educated in South Africa. I am often drawn to the philosophy of Samantha Vice, who suggests that one moral response for white people in South Africa is a certain kind of silence. She argues:

> So, recognizing their damaging presence, whites would try, in a significantly different way to the normal workings of whiteliness, to make themselves invisible and unheard, concentrating rather on those damaged selves. Making pronouncements about a situation in which it is so deeply implicated seems a moral mistake – it assumes one matters politically and morally beyond the ways in which everyone matters equally.[7]

Vice calls her 2010 essay 'How Do I Live in This Strange Place?', evoking the music of a white Afrikaaner boy, Bernoldus Niemand (this pseudonymous name means 'nobody' in Afrikaans), whose music was a weapon in the white anti-apartheid movement. Yet clearly, I have chosen not to be silent. I am as entangled in these contradictions and in these troubling tropes as any producer that I engage with here. How it will end and how I disentangle myself is in many ways the purpose of this book. I have written here very much as a South African, with my own particular but also national struggle over Whiteness and its privileges. While this is a book about Americanness and how it articulates with Whiteness through its love affair with an imagined Africa, it depends on a reading from South African Whiteness.

For a surprisingly long time, South Africans were able to pretend that Whiteness did not need to be at the center of change in the country. Since the fall of the apartheid regime and its formal structures of white supremacy, white privilege in South Africa has been almost entirely unacknowledged and unseen by most white South Africans. It is woven in the fabric of South African life in ways that we imagine are obvious and yet slip through as class or perhaps even just nasty personalities. For some, like journalist and newspaper editor Ferial Haffajee, whose politics is rooted in an anti-apartheid movement that was founded on a non-racialism born of black consciousness, the study of Whiteness that she observed at the University of

Johannesburg' Whitewash conference in March 2013[8] was a distraction. She expresses frustration that anybody in South Africa would be paying attention to Whiteness, let alone that there would be an academic study based on the need to denaturalize Whiteness. She saw this conference as just another version of white's claiming victimization and another way of undermining the lessons of the anti-apartheid movement and black consciousness.[9] Her frustration led her to ask "What if there were no Whites in South Africa?", the title of her book. Her provocative question, however, was necessary to show, as she does, how Whiteness sticks through systems of cultural, linguistic and stylistic expectations, through capitalist structures and western political systems, whether there are any white people around or not.[10] Jemima Pierre evokes this kind of racecraft in *The Predicament of Blackness*, where she articulates the idea of race as a set of historically structured institutions, as well as cultural phenomena in a country like Ghana.[11] These mask the extent to which white power and privilege is rooted in colonial and imperial structures that continue to dominate African geopolitics and economics. As Haferjee explores wealth and power in South Africa, she exposes these kinds of neocolonial structures that make white supremacy possible even when Black people are in power.

I suggest that at the heart of this paradox – our need to make Whiteness central because it is already too central – is the way that Whiteness performs itself even as it interrogates itself through satire and theater. Despite the times and the occasional banning and shuttering of certain artists and performances during the 1970s and 1980s, white South Africans could go to the theater to either laugh at the ridiculousness of the apartheid regime or feel outside of the worst aspects of that regime. Evita Bezuidenhout was a character in Pieter-Dirk Uys' drag performances that played to white audiences in South Africa. Evita was the South Africa government's ambassadress to the fictional homeland of Bapetikosweti and was the center of a number of satirical plays such as *Adapt or Dye* (1982), *Skating on Thin Uys* (1985) and *Beyond the Rubicon* (1986).[12] From the 1970s well into the 1990s, she skewered the apartheid regime and its acolytes around the world. Evita was so famous she had her own talk show in the 1990s interviewing not just Nelson Mandela but the architect of the negotiations and now president, Cyril Ramaphosa and the head of the then new African National Congress government's Reconstruction and Development Plan, Jai Naidoo, among others. The astute and fabulous comedy of Pieter-Dirk Uys and the other searing and brilliant playwrights and actors, black and white, attempted to disturb the complacence of white South Africans. Not to take anything away from them, however, it was remarkable how little the apartheid regime cared.

In *Performing Whitely in the Postcolony*,[13] Megan Lewis uses performances by Afrikaaners during and after apartheid to ask hether Whiteness can unpack its own privilege. Uys, as Lewis shows, like many satirists, was very successful in using incongruity, ambiguity and language to queer a deeply patriarchal regime and frame Whiteness and its privileges ironically.[14] He could do this because in repressive regimes satire protects the performer from the aggression of its objects. Yet as Megan Lewis argues, Uys, and especially Evita, inhabited a dual privilege. As a white man playing a woman, he was able to speak in ways he could not have otherwise, due in part to his success at embodying the mythological figure of maternal authority, the Afrikaans Tannie, a quintessential mother of the nation and of all boys. Here Uys describes in an interview with Daniel Lieberfield in 1997 how he circumvented the many banning orders and threats against him:

> Every time I was really in trouble, I'd get her on the front page of a newspaper wearing some funny hat and looking like an idiot, and everyone would go, "Oh Christ, the drag queen's at it again. Let's move on. It's not worth pursuing." Not taking it seriously, because in fact it was so serious you couldn't even think about it. The atmosphere then was terrifying.[15]

While parody reveals systems of power for what they are so that an audience can recognize them, it depends on familiarity, a familiarity that Lewis suggests allows the audience to feel at a distance from their own complicity. As a woman, Uys could only speak truth to power (if he in fact did) because he was a man! Beyoncé's performative embodying of Yoruba Goddesses does similar work. When she retells the story of the birth of a Black king in Africa but agrees to be the face/body of diamond company Tiffany & Co. by wearing the Hope Diamond,[16] she is embodying both Black power and extractive capitalism in a way that is only possible because white folks love, or at least are comfortable, with her Blackness. Although, not parody, *Black is King* is at least meant to be disruptive, meant to offer a new telling of the story of Blackness when it leaves Africa. But wearing a diamond so closely linked to the pinnacle of Cecil Rhodes and his company De Beer's exploitation of African wealth, just makes it seem, once again, too surreal to be real. Like Pieter-Dirk Uys' satire in apartheid South Africa and *stiob* in late-Soviet Russia, which I described in Chapter 2, her performances do less to undermine the system of power than they illustrate how the regimes' discourses and myths are so powerful that we simply cannot speak outside of their languages. What changes, though, when a white artist tries to do this critical work through the painstaking listening to the other, the working with (other) bodies and minds?

Third World Bunfight (TWB), a South African theatre company, whose director, Brett Bailey, was awarded France's *Chevalier des Arts et des Lettre*, was founded on one of the many theater-as-development projects that were funded during the transition to democracy. These sought to use the arts and theater as a way to educate young Black South Africans in townships and rural areas. For Bailey, these projects became the foundation of a group of actors and performers that he would continue to work with for the next 20 years and more. Bailey's productions like *IpiZombi?* reimagines the real-life minibus crash in 1995 when 12 Black schoolboys were killed. This tragedy produced a violent witch hunt that accused 50 local women of turning the dead boys into zombie slaves. *iMumbo Jumbo* used a similar reimagining of events, this time the 1996 quest by Chief Nicholas Tilana Gcaleka to retrieve the supposed skull of his ancestor, King Hintsa kaPhalo – Paramount Chief of the amaXhosa nation – who had been killed by British colonial forces in 1836. These pieces are vibrant musical mash-ups of South African history, ritual and iconography created as spaces for performers and audiences to work through the violence of the early transition out of apartheid. Bailey's goal was to create theatrical works that turned the theater into a community space where audience and performers interacted and where South Africa's intertwined histories of European and African beliefs could clash and communicate in sometime jarring, sometimes syncretic ways.[17]

After years of successful appearances on the European theater circuit, productive collaborations and performances in South Africa, Zimbabwe, Uganda and the Congo, TWB brought the installation *Exhibit B* to London in the late summer/early autumn of 2014. *Exhibit B* was part theater, part installation, part performance art. First developed in South Africa as *Exhibit A* and then in various European cities, it positions local actors in dioramas telling stories of colonial violence in Africa, as well as current acts of violence from the country where it is being staged.[18] For example, in cities like Brussels, Berlin and Amsterdam in 2013, an actor was duct taped to an airplane seat exposing the torture by immigration agents who had allowed a migrant to suffocate to death on a deportation flight.[19] Other images show a seemingly naked women surrounded by the classic accoutrement of colonial bureaucracies. In each scene actors sit still and do not speak. The audience moves through in a carefully timed and choreographed pattern to gaze on these glimpses into historic and current moments of hideous violence against Black bodies. The actors work and rehearse together to prepare for the violence of the scenes and of the gaze they will experience. They are asked to be silent but to meet the viewers' eyes, to gaze back directly and confidently to an audience that is almost always white and mostly European. As the plethora of interviews, news stories and public events made clear at the time, there was no single way performers thought about the work.[20] I was able to meet up and discuss this experience with performers while they were working with Brett Bailey on a new installation, *Sanctuary* in Lisbon in 2017. For some, this experience was traumatizing, and they were conflicted about the impact it had on them and the audience. For other performers, the work done in a community of actors of color engaging with each other and then with audiences from their own home cities was profoundly empowering.

*Exhibit B* was meant to provoke in the interest of confounding expectations about racialized and oppressed black bodies, and more specifically, the role of the past and present white gaze. But after an article in the *Guardian-UK* newspaper was published about the staging of the show at the Edinburg festival in 2014, calling it a "human zoo", a petition was launched to shut it down.[21] The journalist was citing Director Bailey's description of what the performance was meant to evoke – the horrors of the 19th century 'Human Zoo' exhibitions that are still present in racism and xenophobia today. But the idea of a white director putting Black actors in spaces of anti-black violence was decried. The theater company and the Barbican struggled to address what was in many ways a protest about structural and symbolic racism in British theater in general. Despite many attempts for a variety of different conversations, neither side found a way to speak to each other. London, Paris and Brazilian sites for the performance experienced large protests, and the protests in Paris saw riot police; *Exhibit B* shut down in London and São Paulo. This created dynamic debate online and in multiple news forums in Europe; US bloggers on the continent also jumped in to write about how *Exhibit B* failed as a work of art in terms of distancing the art from an act of violence.[22] What became clear was that the artist's intent to undermine racist violence against black bodies could not justify what for many commentators was an additional exploitation of black bodies.

*Exhibit B* might be seen as an extreme kind of appropriation, one that steals experiences of violence and trauma for one's own interest, the interest of the artist trying to provoke, trying to live with guilt and with remorse. Bailey needed to look again at Brownness and Blackness to solve or relieve that anxiety, as Meghan Lewis has argued about white South African artists' attempts to destabilize their white privilege.[23] Add to this, the interests of a white audience looking to feel the pain so they can forget or disassociate from being implicated in the cause and continuation of this violence. Yet if *Exhibit B* is about the fears and anxieties of a white boy in South Africa trying to face a sense of loss growing up in Africa by examining his Whiteness, what work is Africanness doing for Americans in other sites of performing Blackness?

While it might simply be an artefact of my own interests and my familiarity with Bailey's work, the critiques of it kept coming to mind as I watched *Black is King*. *Black is King*'s set pieces, costume design and styling could be drawn straight from the same basic design for many of the diorama's featured in *Exhibit B*. The careful evocation of colonial era ethnographic film and photography, bodies coated in chalky white paint or ochre, deep orange mud, head pieces of beads or woven hair with cowry shells, long necked women and thick jewelry all position us in an Africa as colonists discovered and invented it.

The similarities between *Exhibit B* and *Black is King* are gut wrenchingly particular and disturbing because in *Exhibit B* we also see the chains, the bars and the duct tape. The violence is clear – something that produced anger from Black audiences – in a way that *Black is King* disguises or ignores. Whiteness in South Africa produces discomfort when it tries to critique its own supremacy. Despite the limitations it faces and the violence it benefits from, performances like *Exhibit B* try to love Africanness in a way that struggles with, rather than denies, the past and present of colonial settlers. I suggest, though, that the popular media that reimagines Black Americans' connections to Africa makes similar mistakes when drawing on different forms of African cultural production but is less willing to face the violence of their representations. The performance of Africa as global Blackness in *Black Panther* and *Black is King* is a reversal, in a way, of South Africans' performance of White privilege. Beyoncé and T'Challa are not deliberately performing white power, but they cannot escape this system of white supremacy. The tropes they exploit risk doing the same work as *Exhibit B*, loving Africa in order to emancipate Whiteness. But attempting to tell the story of African power and beauty as if settlers and western imperialism do not exist does the work of silencing Africans.

It is not accidental that I find it so compelling to think about apartheid era South Africa while trying to understand White supremacy in the 21st century United States, especially in relation to privilege and American imaginings of Africa. The South African apartheid regime was so obviously founded on White supremacy with a clearly visible set of structures and systems through which it had to work hard to maintain its power. The United States, however, has maintained similar forms of anti-black violence while denying white supremacy almost entirely through narratives of freedom and equality. South Africans are struggling to live in a post-settler, post-apartheid country with all its promise and all its inherited violence, and it is perhaps not astonishing to see the same struggles in the United States. Both white saviors in Africa laughing at themselves and Black Americans celebrating a pop culture Africa beyond or outside of colonialism reveal that white supremacy articulated with capitalism does not need white people. Americanness yearns for that moment in the 1990s when South Africans could dream of a different society. While that existed only ephemerally and only in some spaces – and I believe that it manifested in performance and theatrical sites – its ghost haunts the struggle to bring real change to South Africa. But it seems that if Americans ever had that moment of overthrowing a settler government, it is in some ways even more distant and unimaginable. When I wrote *Travel, Humanitarianism, and Becoming America in Africa* I promised, in Cervenak's words, the possibility, not of an end to American geopolitical violence, but rather "the possible establishment of a new ethics that resists the iconographic reductions that enable such violence".[24] Yet Americans continue to look across the Atlantic to Africa to find that hope and to reimagine their future. As long as Americanness depends on silencing Africans or saving them, a shared space of creativity and partnerships will remain elusive.

## Notes

1. Cervenak, Sarah Jane and Kathryn Mathers. 2012. 'The End/s of America.' *Transition*, no. 107: 127–135. https://doi.org/10.2979/transition.107.127.
2. Mathers, Kathryn. 2010. *Travel, Humanitarianism and Becoming American in Africa*. New York, NY: Palgrave/Macmillan.
3. Cervenak, Sarah Jane and Kathryn Mathers. 2012: 134. Ibid.
4. I am grateful for conversations with Ami Shah for underscoring these erasures.
5. Rodríguez, Dylan. 2008. 'Inaugurating Multiculturalist White Supremacy.' *ColorLines*, November 10, 2008. www.colorlines.com/articles/dreadful-genius-obama-moment.
6. See also: "To the extent that the subjection of indigenous, Black, and Brown people to regimes of displacement and suffering remains the condition of possibility for the reproduction (or even the reinvigoration) of an otherwise eroding American global dominance, the figure of Obama represents a new inhabitation of white supremacy's structuring logics of violence". Rodríguez, Dylan. 2008. Ibid.
7. Vice, Samantha. 2010. 'How Do I Live in This Strange Place?' *Journal of Social Philosophy*, 41(3): 323–342, 335.
8. While the conference website or Haferjee's *City Press* article no longer exist online, the events page for WITS University describes the conference as: "'WHITEWASH I' marks the first time that contemporary South African whiteness has been the object of a sustained scholarly enquiry that goes beyond individual research. . . . An overarching thematic of the workshop is the introduction of critical whiteness studies to the South African academy with a view to developing forms of discourse that are particular to whitenesses in post-apartheid South Africa". http://artthrob.co.za/Listings/Conference_at_University_of_Johannesburg_Art_Gallery_in__March_2013.aspx 'WHITEWASH I'. Accessed September 24, 2021.
9. Following Biko's idea of Blackness that included all people of color who identified and recognized themselves as marginalized.
10. Haffajee, Ferial. 2015. *What if There Were No Whites in South Africa?* Johannesburg: Pan Macmillan South Africa.
11. Pierre, Jemima. 2012. *The Predicament of Blackness: Postcolonial Ghana and the Politics of Race*. Chicago: University of Chicago Press.
12. Find descriptions of all his plays on his own website: www.pdu.co.za/.

13. Lewis, Megan. 2016. *Performing Whitely in the Postcolony: Afrikaners in South African Theatrical and Public Life*. Iowa City: Iowa University Press.
14. Lewis, Megan. 2016. Ibid.
15. Lieberfeld, Daniel and Pieter-Dirk Uys. 1997. 'Pieter-Dirk Uys: Crossing Apartheid Lines. An Interview.' *TDR*, 41(1): 61–71, 69.
16. See Tiffany & Co.'s own description of the campaign and of the diamond dug up in Kimberley, South Africa in 1877: www.tiffany.com/stories/guide/beyonce-and-jay-z-about-love/.
17. I have been conducting fieldwork with TWB since 2015 and have watched the development of the company since its formation in the mid-1990s. See also Bailey, Brett. 2003. *The Plays of Miracle & Wonder*. Cape Town: Double Storey Books.
18. See for example: Cervulle, Maxime. 2017. 'Exposer le racisme. *Exhibit B* et le public oppositionnel.' *Études de communication*, 48: 37–54, Flockemann, Miki. 2011. 'Facing the Stranger in the Mirror: Staged Complicities in Recent South African Performances.' *South African Theatre Journal*, 25(2): 129–141, Lewis, Megan. 2018. 'Until You See the Whites of Their Eyes: Brett Bailey's *Exhibit B* and the Consequences of Staging the Colonial Gaze.' *Theatre History Studies*, 37: 115–144, Robles, Fanny. 2018. From Reverse Ethnography to Cultural Performance: Reenacting Colonial Shows in Contemporary France.' *Interventions*, 20(7): 1037–1052.
19. Meerman, Brent. 2014. '"Exhibit B": Look Black in Anger.' *This is Africa*, September 9, 2014. https://thisisafrica.me/politics-and-society/brett-bailey-exhibit-b-look-black-anger/.
20. See commentary here: Greig, Robert. 'Brett Bailey's Exhibit B: Art Could be as Jagged as Broken Glass.' *Daily Maverick*, September 29, 2014. www.dailymaverick.co.za/article/2014-09-29-brett-baileys-exhibit-b-art-could-be-as-jagged-as-broken-glass/#.WhTIozdOmUk. Accessed May 2017, Schutte, Gillian. 2014. 'Brett Bailey's Human Zoo and Discourse Bunfight.' *Mail & Guardian*, September 16, 2014. https://thoughtleader.co.za/the-brett-bailey-human-zoo-and-discourse-bunfight/. Accessed May 2017. For reporting on the event itself: Rucki, Alexandra. 2014. 'Barbican's Exhibit B Closed Down by Protesters Branding Show "Racist".' *Evening Standard*, September 23, 2014. www.standard.co.uk/news/london/barbican-show-exhibit-b-closed-down-by-protesters-branding-performance-racist-9751933.html.
21. O'Mahony, John. 2014. 'Edinburgh's Most Controversial Show: Exhibit B, a Human Zoo.' *The Guardian*, Monday, August 11, 2014. See the petition here: www.change.org/p/withdraw-the-racist-exhibition-exhibition-b-the-human-zoo.
22. Lewis, Megan. 2018. 'Until You See the Whites of Their Eyes: Brett Bailey's *Exhibit B* and the Consequences of Staging the Colonial Gaze.' *Theatre History Studies*, 37: 115–144. http://doi.org/10.1353/ths.2018.0007.
23. Lewis, Megan. 2016. Ibid.
24. Cervenak, Sarah Jane and Kathryn Mathers. 2012: 138. Ibid.

# Index

Abah, Joshua 82
Abebe, Hilina 8
Abu Alala, Amjad 10
Abubakar, Fati 8
Acquah, Nana Kofi 2–3, 8
activism, change 17
*Activist, The* (television series) 61; parody/horror, feeling 63
*Adapt or Dye* (Uys) 102
Adetiba, Kemi 10
Adichie, Chimamanda Ngozi 45
Adjei, Emmanuel 81
adventure tourism: sex tourism, relationship 34–35; study 29–30
Africa: American care, process 15; American encounters 19–20; American imaginings 87, 99; American sentimentality 1; ancestral connection 80–81; change/continuities 20; critical voices, dependence 7–8; culture, richness 27; devastation, colonialism (impact) 92; diasporic voices, conversations/struggles 71; "doing Africa" 34–35; global Blackness performance 106; images, consistency/damage 3–4; imagined Africa, celebration 87; imagining 6–7; imagining, grounding 86; inequalities, image re-creation 21–22; loving 30–31; mobilization 4–5; naming, problem 4–12; neocolonial relationship 99; paradox 9–10; problems, flattening/simplification 29; reimagining 8–12; representational tropes, change (absence) 4; saving 27–28, 31; saving, parody (usage) 42; saving, voluntourists navigation 22–23; thriving 76; un/real Africa 86–90; western power/authority, articulation 17–18
Africa Corps Radi-Aid 2.0 parody 53
*Africa for Norway* (music video) 51–52
*Africa is a Country* (magazine) 87
African artists 82–84
African belonging, erasure 87
African futures/pasts, imaging 84–86
Africanfuturism 88–89
African motifs/motions, extraction 83
African National Congress, students (meeting) 20
Africans: helplessness 47–48; images, alternatives 55–56; urban Africans, influence 81
"African village," backdrop (recognition) 47
African worlds 82–84
"Africa Stop Ebola" *(Africa Contre Ebola)* 44–45
Afrofuturism, celebration 84
agencies, parody 50–53
ahistorical empty space, replacement 78
AIDS testing kits, need 31
Ake, Ibra 81
Akers, Zerina 82
Akinro, Boluwatife 87
Amanze, Chinyere 82
*Amazing Race* (television series) 52
America: belonging 90–93; loving 31; saving 88–89; strictures 5
American: becoming 12, 70; seeing 24–30

American Blackness, Savior Industrial Complex (relationship) 86
American Express, Global Fund donation 17
*American Idol* (television series) 27, 30
Americanness 78, 91; Africa meaning/ideas 2, 5; making, contradictions (impact) 10–11; whiteness, articulation 4; whiteness, link 90
American privilege, Black South African resentment 25–26
Americans: strictures 5; young Americans, transactional neoliberal solution 29
American sentimentality, warning 1–2
anti-Blackness 79
anti-black violence: context 87; forms, maintenance 106–107
apartheid regime 103; fall 101
Apple, Global Fund donation, (RED) 17
*Apprentice, The* (television series) 52
Armani, Global Fund donation, (RED) 17
*Avengers Endgame* (film) 72
Awadi, Didier 44
awareness raising, dependence 62
Ayisi, Erica 79

Bahango, Ekwa 10
Bailey, Brett 103–106
BandAid 30 45; problem 45–46; revival 51
Barbie Paradox 12, 42
Barbie Savior (Instagram account) 12, 36, 54, 63, 100; entanglements 88; humor, usage 59
Bazawule, Blitz 81
"Beyoncé and the Heart of Darkness" (Akinro/Segus-Lean) 87
*Beyond the Rubicon* (Uys) 102
Bezuidenhout, Evita 102
Bibang, Arturo 8
Biddle, Pippa 23
bigotry actions, rights (defense) 26
Black African, embodiment 43
Black America, flattening 78
Black Americanness, stories 11
Black Americans: attacks 11; challenges 25–26; exploitation/violation 92–93; oppression, structural forces (impact) 64; representations 4; struggles, South African struggles (contrast) 25–26
Black bodies, violations 2
black consciousness 101–102
black diaspora 78
Black empire (world domination/subjugation) 92
"Blacker Than You" (Semphere) 64
"black European," shared experience 43
*Black is King* (documentary) 72, 80–85, 87, 100; Africa, global Blackness performance 106; Africa, imagining 86; African belonging, erasure 87; Afrofuturism, celebration 84; erasure site 89; phenomenon 91; set pieces/costume design/styling 105–106; tension, importance 83
Black Is Queen 12, 70
Black lives: centering/valuing 71; saving 90
Black Lives Matter, impact 20
*Black Mirror* (television series) 63
Blackness: emancipation 71; examination 105; global Blackness, celebration 79; global Blackness travel, vocabularies (understanding) 71–72; global community 78; positive representations, creation 64–65; power/beauty 27; story 103
black non-Americans, experience (awareness) 87–88
Black Panther (comic book series) 70, 72–75, 76; anti-Blackness 79
*Black Panther* (film) 72–75, 77, 85, 100; Africa, global Blackness performance 106; African belonging, erasure 87; American struggles, disarticulation 89; costume design, importance 83–84; erasure site 89; phenomenon 91; trope 88
Black people, entanglements 88
Black power, American struggles (disarticulation) 89
Black South Africans: economic challenges 25–26; education 104
*Blind Side, The* (film) 33
Blomkamp, Neill 85
Blumenthal, Neil 33

## Index    111

Bono 52; Africa is burning declaration 88; black man's mask, parody 42–43; (RED) campaign 17
Boomtown Rats 42
Boseman, Chadwick 72
*Bridge, The* (Gluckman) 60
Brownness, examination 105
"Brown Skin Girl" (Rowland) 81
buy one give one (BOGO) 17; companies 32–33

Cameroon citizens, officials (interaction) 60
Campbell, Naomi 81
capitalism, critique 15
*Captain America* (film) 72, 74
*Captain America – Civil War* (film) 74
*Captain Marvel* (film) 72
care: curation 22–24; gendering 35; politics 48
caring: commodification, social media (relationship) 16–17; femininity/consumption, relationship 29; translation 32
caring white women shoppers 31–36
caring white women shopping 54–55
Carter, Blue Ivy 81
celebrity saviors, parody 43–45
Cervenak, Sarah 99,107
Childish Gambino 80
Chopra, Priyanka (*The Activist* host) 62
clicktivism 17, 31; dependence 62
Clooney, George (self-aggrandizement) 45
Cobb, Jelani 78, 79
Coldplay 44
Cole, Teju: tweets 1–2, 11, 17, 45, 90–91; WSIC salience, insistence 63
collective society, construction 19
colonial entanglements 60–61
colonial era films/violence, visual format/reminder 84
colonialism 91, 106; ahistorical empty space, replacement 78; critique 15; existence, journey 91; impact 92
coloniality, active global power 92
colonizer, actor role 77
Comic Relief (2007) 42
Comic Relief UK 46
*Coming 2 America* (film) 76

*Coming to America* (film) 73, 77
*commadement,* ceremonies/rituals (performing) 61
consumption: collapse, white supremacy (impact) 63; femininity/caring, relationship 29
Converse, Global Fund (RED) donation 17
Coogler, Ryan 78, 88
corporate social responsibility, Africa Corps Radi-Aid 2.0 parody 53
COVID-19: images, impact 3; impact 20
cowry shells, importance 82
critical process, silencing 61

Daley-Ward, Yrsa 81
"Danger of a Single Story, The" (Adichie) 45
DEAR TOTO (WordPress blog) 49–50
Democratic Party, students (meeting) 20
Destiny's Child 81
*Devil Came on Horseback, The* (Steidle/Steidle Wallace) 6
diasporic Blackness, Africanfuturism description 88–89
digital social spaces, unevenness 56
*Dinner Party – The Good Guys Christmas, The* (video) 50
DiscoverCorps, saving opportunities 18
Dolezal, Rachel 90
Dooley, Stacy 46
"Do They Know It's Christmas" (song) 44, 51
DukeEngage (paid-for volunteering opportunities) 28

Ebola: epidemic, funds (raising) 44; images, impact 3
Edge, The (parody) 43
Enwezor, Okwui 6
equality, understanding 26
*E.R.* (television series) 30
Esiebo, Andrew 8
ethnographic films, visual format 84
Evans, Hugh 62

Fakoly, Tiken Jah 44
family, valuing 32
Faramelli, Anthony 89
Feed Africa challenge 52–53

femininity: consumption/caring, relationship 29; iconic femininity, translation 35–36
Fishing for Envy 46
Floyd, George (murder) 2, 62–63
Force of Nature (youth advocacy organization) 63
Ford, Tanisha 82
Frankenberg, Ronald 60
Freeman, Martin 77
Frimpong-Manso, Shirley 10

Gabay, Clive 4
Gandhi (video appearance) 50–51
Gap, Global Fund donation (RED) 17
Gcaleka, Nicholas Tilana 104
Geldoff, Bob 42, 44, 45, 52
Gervais, Ricky 42–43
*Get Out* (film) 63–64
Ghana, ethnography exposés 89
*Gift, The* (soundtrack) 72, 80–81
Gilboa, David 33
Giselle (Africa campaign) 44
Gitonga, David 10
global Blackness: Africa, performance 106; celebration 79; focus 87; travel, vocabularies (understanding) 71–72
global capitalist/exploitative economies/institutions, white saviorism (overlap) 2
Global Citizen, apology tweet 62
global equity project 55
Global Fund (RED campaign) 46–47
global inequality, structures/causes 48
Global North, dominance 92
global white supremacy: debate 20; specter, evocation 4
Gluckman, Max 60
good American, formation 11
Greedy Grabby Volunteering 45
*Green Book* (film) 33
Gunnarsdottir, Elsa 23
"Gurl Goes to Africa" (launch) 49–50
Gürsel, Zeynep 4
GVI, voluntourism opportunities 18

Haffajee, Ferial 101–102
Hallmark, Global Fund (RED) donation 17
Harris, Zakiya Dalila 64

*Help, The* (film) 33, 63
Herrman, Cassandra 8, 55
*Hidden Figures* (film) 33
HIV/AIDS epidemic: devastation 11; fight, support 44; impact 15; news domination 16
Hogan, Clover 63
Hope, Clover 81
hopelessness, focus 9
Hough, Juliann (*The Activist* host) 62
"How Do I Live in This Strange Place" (Vice) 101
"How to Write About Africa" (Wainaina) 8
Hubbard, Laura 29, 33, 34
humanitarian brands 99–100
humanitarian concept, essence 86
humanitarian fundraising tropes, parody 52
humanitarian imagery, classics (reproduction) 48
Humanitarian Industrial Complex 4, 58
humanitarian industries, COVID (impact) 16
humanitarianism, foundational narrative (stability) 18
"Humanitarians on Tinder" (launch) 49
Human Sciences Research Council (HSRC), orphan tourism report 45–46
"Humans of New York" (parody) 48–49
"human zoo" 105
humor, usage 59
Hunt, Andrew 33

*I Am Because We Are* (Akunyili-Parr) 6
iconic femininity, translation 35–36
*If Voluntourists Talked About North America* (video) 49–50
images: making/sharing 20–22; traveling images 15; visual images, benign-ness/power 16
imagined Africa, celebration 87
imagined frames, danger 2
Iman (Africa campaign) 44
imperialism 91; Africa (escape) 76; ahistorical empty space, replacement 78
*iMumboJumbo* 104
*In Congo's Shadow* (Linton) 56
Instagram 55, 81

*Invisible Children* (documentary) 6
Invisible Children (nonprofit) 28
*IpiZombi?* 104

Jackson, Samuel L. 64
Jacobs, Sean 56
Jesus (video appearance) 50–51
*Jesus Goes Online* (video) 50–51
Jolie, Angelina 27; self-aggrandizement 45
Jones, James Earl 80
Judge, Ruth Cheung 21

Kagumire, Rosebell 56
Kahiu, Wanuri 10
Kani, John 74
Keep a Child Alive campaign (Keys) 44, 84
Keïta, Salif 44
Keïta, Seydou 8
Kenya, study abroad students (photography choices) 21
Keys, Alicia 44, 84
Kingsley, Mary 34
Knowles-Carter, Beyoncé Giselle (African goddess) 79–86, 103; collaborations 89
*KONY 2012* 28, 31, 45; Kagumire response 56
Kony, Joseph (capture) 28
Kristoff, Nikolas (problem complexity, reduction insistence) 46

*La Maison Noir* (Petit Noir) 83
Lammy, David 46
*Late Night with Seth Meyer* (television series) 33
Lewis, Megan 102–103, 105
LGBTQ+ activism, debate 20
"liberal multiculturalist common sense" 100
*Liberated Threads* (Ford) 82
Lieberfield, Daniel 103
Linton, Louise 54, 56
*Lion King, The* (film) 72, 80, 81
"Lion Sleeps Tonight, The" (Mbube) 80
Live Nation (music production company) 62
Lord's Resistance Army (LRA) 28
Lusting for Likes 46

Madonna, impact 27, 33
Magubane, Peter 8
*Maki'La* (film) 10
*Making the Gift* (documentary) 80–81, 85
Malé, Soungalo 8
Mandela, Nelson 102
"Many Faces of George Floyd, The" (Philips) 64
"Marvel White Supremacy Memo" (Priest) 73
"master and slave" complex 26
Mbembe, Achille 60–61
Mbube ("Lion Sleeps Tonight") 80
McIntosh, Peggy 89
Milford, BOGO effort 32
"Millennials of New York" (social media sendup) 48–49
Minishi, Barbara 8
Moroccan Children's Trust, volunteers interviews 23
Morrow, Andrew 81
Mother Teresa (video appearance) 50
multiculturalism 27
Murphy, Eddie 73, 76
Mutunga, Felix 79
Mycoskie, Blake 33

Naidoo, Jai 102
*Nairobi Half-Life* (film) 10
Ndlovu-Gatsheni 92
Ndlovu, Pinki 92
"nice white lady," description 55, 63
non-racialism 101–102
NORAID, Radiators for Norway campaign 51, 100
Norwegian Students' and Academics' Assistance Fund (SAIH) 51
Ntsele, Solomon 80
Ntsoma, Neo 8
Nyabolo, Nanjala 79
Nyong'o, Lupita 81

Obama, Barack 100
Okorofor, Ndedi 88–89
Oliver, Jaime 42
One Direction 44
*One Girl's Perilous Journey to the Heart of Africa* (Linton) 54
*Onion, The* (satirical challenges) 48

## 114  Index

oppression, shared histories 87–88
optimism, value (extolling) 54
orphan tourism report, Human Sciences Research Council (HSRC) 45–46
*Other Black Girl, The* (Harris) 64
*Out of Africa* 85; Blixen fantasy 30

Pailey, Bobby 28
Pailey, Robtel 45
Paltrow, Gwyneth 44
Pan-Africanism 89–90
Parker, Sarah Jessica 44
parodic whiteness 63
parody: agencies, parody 50–53; celebrity saviors, parody 43–45; critique, power 61; limits 56–59; overidentification 61; problem insight 45–46; responses 46–48; satirical challenges 48–50; usage 42; WSIC self-reinvention 90–91
"passing for white" 25
Peace Corps, impact 18
people, relationships (spatialization) 60
*Perfect Picture, The* (film) 10
*Performing Whitely in the Postcolony* (Lewis) 102
Petit Noir 83
phenotypical whiteness, Whiteness (contrast) 4
Philips, Maya 63, 64
physical violence, acts 64–65
Pierre, Jemima 9, 89–90, 102
political institutions, postcolony force participation 61
Poole, Laren 28
poor countries, Americans/Europeans interaction (history) 18
pop culture spaces, function 71
postcolonial entanglements 60–61
poverty 91; focus 9
Pratt, Mary Louise 34
*Predicament of Blackness, The* (Pierre) 102
pre-modern Africa, iconography 84
Priest, Christopher 70, 72, 73, 77, 88
Promote Africa challenge 52–53
public ceremonies, impact 60

race, seeing 24–30
racial divide, transcending 70
racial inequalities, remedies 24
racial thinking 24
racism: integralness 64–65; intolerance 26; US racism, context 87
racist structures, influence 92–93
Radiators for Norway campaign (NORAID) 55, 100; taglines 53; videos 51–53
Ragingly Enlightened Wrath 46
Raider, Jeffrey 33
Ramaphakela, Katleho 10
Ramaphakela, Rethabile 10
Ramaphosa, Cyril 102
RED campaign 99–100; Bono launch 17; caring, translation 32; "UNITE to FIGHT" 47; videos, focus 47–48
Red Nose Day 46
RED Revolution 2020 47–48
*Reductress* (online magazine) 48
Reed, Aldous 90
representation, styles (changes) 35
Research Slothery 45–46
Riise, Anja Bakken 51
Rodríguez, Dylan 100
Rojek, Chris 61
romance tourism, engagement 34–35
Rowland, Kelly 81
Roy, Ishita 32
Russell, Jason 28

*Sanctuary* (installation) 104–105
satire: collapse, white supremacy (impact) 3; WSIC self-reinvention 90–91
satirical challenges 48–50
satirical hypernormalization, dependence 90–91
Savior Industrial Complex, American Blackness (relationship) 86
saviorism: politics 48; white American laughter 100
savior, shopper (impact) 35
Schwarz, Kaylin 21, 24
Seal (Africa campaign) 44
Segus-Lean, Joshua 87
self-awareness: display 9; importance 23
self, definition 87–88
Semphere, Priscilla Takondwa 64, 86–88

sentimental celebrity, persistence (appeal) 44–45
*Seriously Single* (film) 10
Serkis, Andy 74
service-learning credit, absence 19
Seven African Powers, Orishan idea 82
sex tourism, adventure tourism (relationship) 34–35
Shaffer, Claire 81
Sheeran, Ed 44
Shire, Warsan 81
"Shirley Valentine syndrome" 34–35
shopper, impact 35
shopping for caring 32–33
shopping for good 16–17; comfort zone 35
"shop until it stops" effort 17
Sidibé, Malick 8
Sihlengeni Secondary School 47
single story photographs, danger 3
Sissako, Abderrahmane 10
*Skating on Thin Uys* (Uys) 102
slactivism 17, 31
Snapchat 55
socially engaged travel, student plan/questions 23
social media: caring commodification, relationship 16–17; platforms, African usage 44–45; profiles, engagement 19; rise, impact 17; tone, summarization 50; travel photographs, trend 21
South Africa: Black South Africans, economic challenges 25–26; HIV/AIDS epidemic, impact 15; racist history/racism 24–25; struggles, Black American struggles (contrast) 25–26; students, interviews 15–16; wealth/power, exploration 102
southern African, Americans (travel/visit) 18–19
students: interviews/fieldwork 19; transformational experiences 15–16
"suffering Africans" 42
superhero, black actor role 72
*Survivor Africa* (television series) 29–30; AIDS charity, launch 31
systematic racism 63

Tanzania, voluntourist (Biddle experience) 23
"Tarzan" (imperialist narrative) 78
Taylor, Liz 44
TeachAmerica, impact 18
Tesfaye, Gabrielle 78
Third World Bunfight (TWB) 7, 103–104
*Timbuktu* (film) 10
tokenism, rise 56
TOMS shoes, BOGO effort 17, 32, 33
transracial identity, Dolezal claim (problem) 90
travel (change), COVID (impact) 16
travelers: examination 15–16; self-representations, carefulness 24
*Travel, Humanitarianism, and Becoming American in Africa* (Mathers) 1, 6, 10, 16, 99, 107; Africa, caring methods (change) 16–17; stories 20
traveling images 15
Trump, Donald (shit-hole countries) 73
Tucker, Boima 78
Twain, Mark 54
Twitter, mission 55–56

unbearable whiteness 89–90
*Uncle Sam* (Abah) 82
UNICEF Sweden videos 50–51
United States: citizen responsibility 25; multiculturalism 27; racist history 24
University of Johannesburg, Whitewash conference 102
un/real Africa 86–90
urban Africans, influence 81
Usher (*The Activist* host) 62
US racism, context 87
Uys, Pieter-Dirk 102–103

verbal violence, acts 64–65
Vice, Samantha 101
Villasana, Daniella 3
violence, focus 9
*Virunga* (documentary) 6
visual images, benign-ness/power 16
Volunteering as Gluttonous Consumption 45–46
voluntourism 17–19, 100; critiques 59; impact 6, 16–17; industry, absence

19; industry, growth 18; problems 45–46
voluntourists: Africa navigation 22–23; learning/care curating 22–24; questions 23; studies 19
*Vulture* (Priest) 73

Wainaina, Binyavanga 8–9, 30, 54
Wakanda, American (becoming) 12, 70
Warby Parker, BOGO effort 17, 32
*War Dance* (documentary) 6
war mongering 91
"War on Terror" 27
"We Are the World 25" (remake) 51
WeChat 55
western colonialism, Africa (escape) 76
western power/authority, articulation 17–18
*What Are We Doing Here?* (documentary) 6
WhatsApp 55
*When I Say Africa* (film/photographs) 7–10, 19, 55, 85; Biddle, interlocutor 23
white aesthetic, African American struggles 82
white man's burden 77
whiteness: Americanness, articulation 4; Americanness, link 90; centrality 33; grounding 90; importance, absence 101–102; mocking 90–91; parodic whiteness 63; "passing for white" 25; power, hypernormalization 101; structural forces, impact 64; success 62–65
Whiteness, phenotypical whiteness (contrast) 4
white privilege 64; questioning 4
white savior: becoming (process) 29–30; entanglements 88
white savior complex: cultural/political critique 23; meme 46

White Savior Industrial Complex (WSIC): Americanness dependence 4; Cole insistence, importance 63; Cole tweets 45; creation 12; critique 33; critique, feminization/entanglement 71; evocation 89; founding 33–34; making/sustaining 16–17; paradox 6; parodic critique 12, 55; penetration/extraction ability 35; privilege, validation 2; remaking 8; self-reinvention 90–91; sustaining 100; violence, blurring 29; warning 1
white saviorism: critiques, paradox 6; global capitalist/exploitative economies/institutions, overlap 2
white supremacy 106; consumption/satire collapse 63; disruption 101; formal structures 101; questions 27
white victimization, claim 102
Whitewash conference (University of Johannesburg) 101–102
White Woman Consumer 35–36
*Who Wants to be a Millionaire* (television series) 52
Winfrey, Oprah (impact) 27, 33, 90–91
Workin' Pride 45–46
World Nomad, voluntourism opportunities 18
*Worlds Apart* (television series) 32
World Vision, appeals 52

Yoruba goddesses, imagining 80
young Americans, transactional neoliberal solution 29
*You Will Die at 20* (film) 10

Zamunda 73, 75–78
Zibi, Tina 8
Zohn, Ethan 31
Zulus, integration 60
Zylla, Manfred 15

For Product Safety Concerns and Information please contact our EU representative  GPSR@taylorandfrancis.com
Taylor & Francis Verlag GmbH, Kaufingerstraße 24, 80331 München, Germany

www.ingramcontent.com/pod-product-compliance
Lightning Source LLC
Chambersburg PA
CBHW051754230426
43670CB00012B/2290